More Hours in My Day

EMILIE BARNES

HARVEST HOUSE PUBLISHERS
Eugene, Oregon 97402

MORE HOURS IN MY DAY

Copyright © 1982 by Harvest House Publishers
Eugene, Oregon 97402

Library of Congress Catalog Card Number 82-081650
ISBN 0-89081-355-8   Trade
ISBN 0-89081-706-5   Mass

Printed in the United States of America.

DEDICATION

This book is dedicated to my husband, Bob, who has loved me for over 27 years. He has continued to encourage and teach me in the Lord and in our home. I thank him for making it possible to keep our home my priority and still letting me be me in the ministry of "More Hours In My Day" seminars.

I thank my mother, who is at home with the Lord, for the domestic-engineering education she gave me as I was growing up. And I thank her for seeing the qualities in Bob as she allowed me to marry him at 17 years of age.

Bob has motivated me to organize and be creative in our home and with our children, Brad and Jenny.

Together we complement each other, all because of Bob's faithfulness to our Lord and his honest and manly spirit. He is truly a man after God's own heart. And because of that we are together in a full-time ministry of teaching God's principles to those whom God brings into our lives through "More Hours In My Day" seminars.

FOREWORD

When Emilie and I first met, in 1974, we were delighted to have found each other. We were the only two people we knew who loved decorating our homes, entertaining company, cooking gourmet meals, managing our households, raising our children, teaching Bible studies, counseling women, and speaking about all of it. At that time my husband, Fred, and I were conducting marriage seminars, and the men were constantly telling us what they wished their wives knew. One day Fred suggested, "Why don't you and Emilie write a course teaching women what their husbands want them to know?"

We both got excited over the prospects and began to prepare outlines for our first "Feminar." As we watched reactions we pruned our material, and as we discovered the needs we developed new ideas. The first time Emilie systematically emptied her handbag, showing the ladies all she had in there, I knew she'd hit a winner! Every woman went home and organized her handbag. When we demonstrated how to make tablecloths out of sheets, the ladies ran for the white sales. As Emilie explained how to organize an entire house in 12 cardboard boxes, women fought to buy boxes.

Soon Emilie put together a new seminar on time management called "More Hours In My Day," and women have been flocking to learn from her ever since.

You will enjoy this book and be thrilled when you and your family see the results of your actions. I know from personal experience that everything Emilie writes works, and she lives what she teaches, for her home and her family are exciting examples.

Florence Littauer

CONTENTS

More Hours in My Day

1
A LOVE STORY

September is the time of year when our children go back to school and we think of all the excitement and fun they have had all summer and of preparing them to return to school. I always look at this as a time of vacation for us. I always said that when September came that's when my vacation began, because the children got back to school and it sort of gave me a time to get scheduled and organized again and have some time for me.

One of the things I recall the most about back-to-school was the time when our daughter began her first year in college. We have two children, a married daughter and a son in college. What happened to me that first year when Jenny started to college was really new and exciting for me. However, being away from home was a little different experience for her. After she had completed her first semester away at school, I got a letter from her that I will never forget.

The Letter Home

Dear Mom:

Since I've been away at college now one full semester I think it's about time that I bring you up-to-date as to what's been going on. Shortly after I arrived at college I got bored with dormitory life and stole $10.00 out of my roommate's purse. With the money I rented a Honda bike and crashed into a telephone pole a few blocks from the college. I broke my leg but was rescued by the young doctor who lives upstairs in the apartment house at the corner. He took me in, nursed me back to good health, and set my leg. Thanks to him I'm up and around again. I wanted to let you know that we're going to get married as soon as possible, but it seems as though we're having some trouble on the blood tests, since there's been a disease that keeps showing up. We do hope, however, that we will be married before the baby arrives and will be home shortly thereafter to live with you and Dad. I know that you will love the baby as much as you have me, even though he will be of a different religion, but, Mom, will you please try to understand all this? The reason that we're having to come home and stay is that my doctor friend flunked out of medical school because of all the attention he was giving me in my condition.

Really, Mom, I didn't steal $10.00 out of my roommate's purse or rent a Honda bike. I didn't hit a telephone pole and break my leg. I didn't meet a young doctor of a different religion, nor are we going to be married. There is no blood test or disease to worry about, or any baby coming along. I won't be home to live with you and Dad, and he won't be either. I am getting a D in geometry and F in geology, however, and I wanted you to accept these grades in their proper perspective.

I think we as moms and women get things out of perspective, don't we? We get so tied up with life and so busy that we sometimes lose what our real priorities are and what our real perspectives in life should be.

Emilie's Roots

I was raised in a Jewish home. My father was orphaned as a very young child in Vienna. As they would often do with orphans, they placed him in an area where he would learn a vocation. And so my father had the wonderful experience of being raised in the palace in Vienna in the kitchen. Later he came to America as a very fine Viennese chef. He met a beautiful young woman 29 years old, with big black eyes and long, black, shiny hair. (My father was 11 years older than my mother.) They were married, and my mother always had the desire of being a homemaker and having a family. but it wasn't until my mother was 38 years old that I was born into the family, although I do have a brother who is a couple of years older than I.

When I was 11 years old my father became very ill and passed away with a coronary. He had been ill for about two years off and on, and we had a lot of doctor's bills and hospital bills that had occurred because of his illness. But we didn't have any insurance, and so Mother was left with two almost-teenage children and a lot of debts to pay. She didn't know exactly how she was going to do all this, but, I have an aunt and uncle who absolutely adored our little family. My aunt and uncle never had any children of their own, and they always thought of us as their little family. So, my aunt and uncle loaned my mother money to open a dress shop. (She had always had the desire to own a dress shop. She had designed and made tennis dresses in her earlier years for the movie stars in the San Fernando Valley.) Mom had a real flair for sewing and tailoring, so she opened this tiny dress shop, and we lived in three rooms behind that store.

At 11 years of age, I found myself beginning my education in what I call "domestic engineering." My mother began to teach me and train me, and I took on the responsibility of those three little rooms. I did the washing and ironing, I planned the meals, I prepared the meals, I shopped for the meals. While I was going to school my mother was teaching me the dress business, and I was very conscientious about it because I felt it was very important to help our family at that time. And so we were able to get ourselves out of debt. We moved to a larger location where we had a little apartment that was away from the dress shop.

The New Model

At that time I was about 15 years old. I had never had a date, and in fact I really didn't look at boys and boys didn't really look at me up to that point. One of the reasons was because of the way I looked. I had brown pigtails piled on top of my head with two big red bows. It isn't just any boy who wants to take out a girl who looks like a fire truck! It was also at about this time in my life that my mother decided she wanted to do some fashion shows in the local restaurant during the lunch hour. The cheapest way to get a model was to send her daughter, Emilie, off to modeling school. So one night a week I went to modeling school. You can imagine what they thought that first night when I walked in with these two big red bows on top of my head! I'm sure they thought, "If we can do something with her, our school is certainly going to be a success!" So the bows got thrown out, the pigtails came down, and the hair got cut. And I will admit it looked better.

While I was there I met a beautiful girl by the name of Esther. Esther was what you would call a natural beauty, and a natural model. She would get on the ramp and just slither along, she was so graceful and charming and at ease. The rest of us would get on the ramp and just sort of klunk along after her. Esther later went to New York City, became a high-fashion model, and was on the cover of many fashion magazines.

Boy-Attracter

One of the things I liked about Esther was that she was what you would call a boy-attracter. I thought that if I got to be good friends with her, maybe somehow I could get myself a date. Well, we became friends, but she lived out of town, so I invited her to stay with me a couple of weeks during the summer. I said, "While you're with me we can play fashion show and have all sorts of fun in my mother's dress shop. But by the way, let's make a little agreement: If you get a date during the two weeks you're staying with me, let's say you have to get me a date, and if I get a date, then I get you a date." I had never had a date, so I figured something was going to work one way or the other.

And you know, that's exactly what happened! We went to the local movie house, and, as many of the teenagers would do during the intermission, we would congregate in the lobby and introduce each other to our friends. That evening I met some friends that I was going to school with, and I introduced them to Esther. They thought she was just beautiful and they wanted to introduce her to some other friends who they were with, so we were introduced to these other friends, who in turn introduced us to some other friends. This one particular young man looked at her and just couldn't take his eyes off her. (It was a legitimate introduction, not just a pickup.) The young man said to her, "I'd really like to take you out," but Esther said, "That'll be fine, but you'll have to get a date for my girl friend, Emilie." He took one look at me and said, "I'll give you a call and

I'll see what I can do." He called the next day and said, "You know, Esther, I just can't find a date for your girl friend, Emilie." She replied, "I'm sorry, then, but I won't be able to go out with you." He answered, "Well, I have an identical twin brother who owes me a favor. Maybe he'll take her out."

The Twin Brother

And, sure enough, his twin brother became my blind date. His name was Bob Barnes, and to this day he says that I was the date and he was blind. But that was the beginning of a marvelous summer romance. We just had a wonderful time all summer long. We went beaching, bicycling, picnicking, and partying.

September was coming, and we were both going to be going back to school, when Bob discovered I had lied to him. I was going to be starting my junior year in high school, and he was going to be starting his senior year in college. He wasn't about to go back and tell his fraternity brothers and all his friends that he had been robbing the cradle all summer with this little junior in high school. So he said to me, "Emilie, you've just been so much fun all summer and we've just had a great time, but I'll see you around." Well, you know what happens to a young girl when her heart is broken. Here was something I wanted, and then when I realized I couldn't have it, I wanted it even more. Well, Bob went back to college, looked over the campus and all the new girls that came in, and decided that there wasn't anyone he would rather see than me. So we began to see each other again.

At 16 years old, I was in love. How could I know at 16 years old that I was in love? Well, I'd been around adults most of my life. By this time I was taking care of our family's little apartment, plus modeling, plus working in my mother's dress shop, plus going into Los Angeles to help my mother do the buying at least once a month, plus going to school. I could easily take care of a home and a family or a husband or whatever. I knew I was in love!

What is a Christian?

One evening, after Bob and I had been on a date, he brought me home to our little apartment and we sat down on the sofa in our living room. He got real serious as he took his hands and held my face in them. He looked me right in the eye and said, "Emilie, I love you, but I cannot ask you to marry me." I certainly couldn't understand that. I loved him and he loved me. Wasn't that the most important thing between two people? Then he said to me, "Emilie, you know that I'm a Christian." Well, I knew he was a Gentile, but a Christian? What is a Christian, anyway? Bob said to me, "A Christian is a person within whom Christ dwells." I replied, "Who is Christ?" And he answered, "Let me explain it to you this way, Emilie. If God wanted to communicate with His people, how would He do it? If there were a snail crawling along and you wanted to talk with that snail, how would you do it? You'd have to become a snail, wouldn't you?" He continued, "That's what God did. He became a Person in His Son, Jesus Christ. He came on this earth to love and teach His people." Then Bob added, "Emilie, most of all He came to die for our sins—your sins and my sins, and the world's sins."

I looked at Bob Barnes and I said, "That's wonderful and that's fine, but I'm not a sinner." Some of you may recognize that you're sinners, but I had been a good girl all my life. I had minded my mother and done all the things I was supposed to do. I had been to Hebrew school and was confirmed. I was a good little Jewish girl. I believed in God. Then Bob said to me, "Do you know what sin is? Sin is when you say that you want to lead your own life, to go your own way, and make your own decisions, and not even acknowledge God for those decisions in your life." And that's exactly what I had been doing. I had been living my life for me, myself, and I. Bob continued, "Emilie, God loves you so much that He actually went to the cross for your sin." Romans 3:23 says, "All have sinned, and fall short of the glory of God." Romans 6:23 says, "The wages of sin is death, but the gift of God is eternal life through Jesus Christ our Lord." I guessed maybe I was a sinner because I was included in that "all." Then Bob said, "Emilie, that's why God sent His Son. He went on that cross, He took the sins of the world, any you've every committed in the past, and you'll ever commit in the future, and any you're involved in right now. He went to that cross and took those upon Himself. He suffered the punishment of hell for you and me. By believing in Him we will never have to experience that ourselves. By receiving Him and letting Him live His life through us, we will never have to experience that. God has done it for us."

Opening the Door

Then Bob said, "In Revelation 3:20, Christ says, 'Behold, I stand at the door and knock. If anyone hears my voice and opens that door, I'll come in. I'll fellowship with you and you can fellowship with me.' " Bob continued, "Emilie, that doorknob is on the inside of your heart. You have to be the one to open and invite Him to come in, and when you do, that's what makes you a Christian. Eternity begins at the moment you open that door and receive Jesus Christ into your life. When we die, it's merely a change of address."

I knew that I loved Bob, and I knew he was the kind of man I wanted to marry, but I had to make some decisions of my own in my life. As he left that night, he told me that he loved me, that he would be praying for me, and that he would trust God for my life.

Well, I knew I was in love with Bob Barnes, and I knew that if I didn't become a Christian I wouldn't be able to marry the man I loved, but I was also smart enough to know that I couldn't just fake it and say I was a Christian the rest of my life. It would have to be real or not at all. So that night, as I went to bed, I said a prayer to God, in my own words, for the first time in my life. I said, "God, I don't understand all this, but if you did have a Son and His name is Jesus, and if He is the Messiah that our people are waiting for, then I want to open the door of my heart and I want You to come in and dwell in me. But, God, I want You to prove it to me."

I thought I was going to get a letter the next day in the mail from God, and I thought it was going to say something like this: "Dear Emilie, I did have a Son, His name is Jesus, and He is your Messiah, so believe in me." But God doesn't always work that way, does He? I began to think that maybe it wasn't Bob Barnes that I was in love with: maybe it was Jesus Christ in him that was so special in this young man's life. During all the many times I had been invited into their home, never once did his family ever say anything to me about being of a different faith. But they loved me and were concerned for me, and of course today I know that they were praying for me. They were praying that God would be revealing Himself in a mighty way in my life.

And it was happening. Miracles were happening and I didn't even recognize them. One was that my mother allowed me to date a Gentile, and then after I told Bob about the prayer I had prayed and asked God to prove it to me, He knew that God would. We didn't know how it was going to happen, but I began to go to church with him. That was the second miracle that happened in my life—that my mother allowed me to go to church with him.

Bob and Emilie

My mother wanted me to marry a doctor or an attorney, to live on a high hill, drive a big fancy car, and wear lots of diamonds. To her that was success. But success comes in other ways, doesn't it? And so she said to me, "Emilie, I'd like to send you to one of the finest finishing schools in Europe. I'd like to give you a car, a wardrobe, and an unlimited expense account if you'll not marry this young man." Well, that's everything in the world a 16-year-old would ever love to have. But, it was as that very moment that God proved to me that I had in my heart God's free gift, our Messiah, Jesus Christ. And I was able to say to my sweet mama, "I love you, but I'd like to marry the young man that I'm in love with, and together we're going to begin to establish a Christian home."

So Bob and I were married. I was starting my senior year in high school and he was starting his first year of teaching. In fact, he used to have to sign my report cards for me! Three years after we were married our daughter Jenny was born, and a few months after Jenny was born, we discovered that we were going to be parents to three more children. How were we going to do that? Well, in the meantime, my brother had gotten married and had had three precious little children, two little girls and a little boy. One day the mommy of these precious little children walked out of the house and never came back. This absolutely destroyed my brother. He couldn't handle the fact that the wife he loved, the mother of his three children, was to leave, only to be seen one time after that. But, God had a pattern for my life. God knew that the time was going to come when I needed every bit of experience that I had in taking care of a home and in handling responsibilities, because now I was going to become the mother of four children under four years old.

Five to Learn From

We took those precious little children into our home, and everything was fabulous. I had everything pulled together: I had those little kids spiffed up, I was making clothes for them, I did the washing, the ironing and the food planning, and the house was in order. I was absolutely superwoman for about a month, until we discovered that I was pregnant. Number five. Then our son Brad was born, so now we had five children under five years old, and I was 21. But God has a pattern for our lives, and He knew that the day would come when I would be teaching women. Titus 2:3, 4 tells us that the older women are to teach the younger women. Never in a million years did I think I would ever be an older woman, but I needed that experience. I needed to be able to identify with women today as they come into my classes, so that I'm able to say that I know what they're going through. I know the heartache, I know the weariness that they experience.

God's Plan for Mother

Well, everything seemed to go well. My brother married a lovely girl who had two children from a previous marriage. They took their three children, so together they had five children. And there we were, the perfect all-American family with a son and a daughter, only to discover shortly afterward that my mother was going bankrupt in her business. God had a pattern for her life. It absolutely stripped her of everything. She had no money, had no car, she had no home, she had nothing. So Bob and I went to my mother and asked her if she would like to come and live with us until she felt she could get back on her feet again.

At this point in my mother's life she was in her early 60's. It's not easy for a woman to go out and try to find a job and make a career for herself at that age. But God had provided for her until her little family got in their little nest and got comfortable and settled. And then everything was taken away. And so we went to pick up my mother to live in our home with us.

As Bob put her little suitcases in the car and helped her into the car, he said to her, "On Sunday we go to church, and we'd like you to go to church with us." I didn't know he was going to say that to my little Jewish mother. And I didn't know what she would say to him, but she didn't say anything. On Sunday morning she was ready to go to church with us. For the next two years Mother lived in our home with us, and every Sunday she was in church with us. And then we discovered one day that my mother, at 65 years of age, had opened the door of her heart and invited our Messiah, Jesus Christ, to come in.

My precious mother grew in the Lord, and at 78 years of age she changed her address from earth to heaven. Today she is with our Lord and our Messiah, Jesus Christ, and I have the sure hope of knowing that someday we will be together.

God's Plan for You

Do you have life in its proper perspective? Do you know that if you were to change your address what that address might be? I pray that God might help you evaluate that decision in your life. You know whether Jesus Christ is knocking on the door of your heart. Your hands might get a little clammy, and your heart might start beating real fast, but this could very well be His call in your life. Don't put Him off with phony excuses. Say yes to the Lord Jesus Christ today.

2

DAILY SCHEDULING

God really did a number on me when I was growing up, because He prepared me for being able to work with women today—to identify with you, to know that you have these struggles in your lives, and to help you be organized.

How do you take care of all these children and your husband and still keep your priorities in order and glorify the Lord? It's difficult. There's no doubt about it. So we're going to talk about how we can do that—how we can actually have more hours in our day. We're going to work with what God tells us about how we can have more hours in our day, and also how to be the type of woman that God wants us to be.

The Night Worker

We're going to start with our daily routine, and how we get started daily in doing these things and in working them out in our lives. We're going to start with Proverbs 31:17, 18, where God tells us that the virtuous woman is energetic and a hard worker, watches for bargains, and works far into the night. If we work far into the night, I guess that means we're going to have to start the night before in order to get ourselves together for the following day. Some of you are saying, "I've got a 24-hour job." You do, absolutely. If you have children at home, you are working 24 hours a day. Some of you were probably up three or four times last night with a sick baby. There's no doubt that God knows what he's talking about when He says you work far into the night, especially if you're a working woman. Your time is short at home, but being organized will help free you from guilt feelings about a messy home. So we're going to start the night before.

One of the ways in which you can do this is by gathering your wash and your laundry and sorting it out. A lot of these things you'll be able to teach your children to do. I encourage you to do that. The children were with us for approximately four years. But during the time they were growing up, we wanted to give them as much responsibility as they could possibly handle at the youngest age they could handle it. This way they were not only working in our home as a family but also learning. By the time they got a little older we didn't have to teach them. We didn't have to worry, because they already knew how to do these things.

One of these things is gathering the wash the night before. Take a piece of fabric (a remnant or whatever—something with alot of color in it) and make a laundry bag about 20 inches wide by 36 inches high. You might want to use a king-sized pillowcase with a shoelace strung through the top. Then say to your little one, "Okay, we're going to play a game."

The Laundry Game

Don't tell them it's work. By the time they're ten they realize you've been working them to death, but they don't know it when they're little, so don't tell them. Say, "We're going to play a game, and it's called sort-the-laundry." Then get out your laundry bag that has lots of colors and says, "This is the bag where all the dirty clothes that have a lot of colors go. Now find something in this dirty-clothes pile that has a lot of colors." So they run over and pick it up, and you say, "Right! Now put it in the colored laundry bag." So they put it in there.

Then make a bag that is navy blue or dark brown and tell them, "This is where all the dark-colored clothes go." This would be the blue jeans, the brown T-shirts, the navy-blue socks—all those dark-colored clothes. "Now run over and find something that's dark-colored." You see, you're playing a game with them. They do it, and you say, "Great! That's absolutely right!" Then you make a bag that's all white, and you say, "Now this is where the white dirty clothes go—the white T-shirts, the white socks, the white underwear, and those things. They go into the white laundry bag.

Now you're going to give them a little rest. You say, "Okay, now find me something that's colored." They run over and pick it up. And then, "Find something that's white." And they put it into the proper bag. What you're doing now is actually teaching a four-year-old how to sort the laundry. When they're six and seven and ten, do you ever have to teach them again? No, because you've already taught them once. Somebody once said to me, "Well, when they're 15 you have to teach them again, because when they're 15 they don't want to do anything. They're that weird teenage group." But at least they know basically how to do it, and they'll come back to it again later on.

Bags and More Bags

Another thing I did which really worked out well was to make individual laundry bags for each of the kids to hang in their room behind their door or in their closet. The other three colored laundry bags could go by your washing machine, in the garage or the service porch or the basement or wherever you happen to have it. I made individual bags that were very colorful that could match the kids' rooms. This is where they put their own dirty clothes. Then whosever job it was for the week to sort the laundry merely went around, collected everybody's laundry bag, and sorted it into the individual laundry bags.

One gal gave me a great idea, which I think is fantastic if your have the room. Go out and buy three of those plastic trash cans in different colors, and put them in the garage. You can label them white clothes, dark clothes and colored clothes with a felt-tip pen. Then your kids can sort the clothes by playing a basketball game with the clothes and trying to hit the right containers.

When summer comes and it's time for them to go off to camp, you can use the laundry bag as a duffel bag. You stick in their sleeping bag, their pillow, their hiking boots, and whatever. If any of you know what it looks like when they dump the sleeping bags into a pile at camp, there's this big pile of nothing but sleeping bags—they all look the same. The kids can't even remember their own name, let alone what their sleeping bag looks like, when they get off the camp bus. But our kids had lived with those laundry bags all year, so they knew what they looked like. They would pick out their laundry bag within a second, and they were relaxed and all set, ready for a week at camp. This way Mom solved a problem at camp even though she wasn't even there!

The Daily Work Planner Chart

Now take a good look at the Daily Work Planner Chart. What we would do, especially when we had the five children, was to take all the chores for the week and put them in a basket. Then we would go around one by one and allow the children to choose—to pick

DAILY WORK PLANNER CHART

DAY OF THE WEEK	MOM	DAD	#1 CHILD	#2 CHILD	#3 CHILD	#4 CHILD	#5 CHILD
SATURDAY							
SUNDAY							
MONDAY							
TUESDAY							
WEDNESDAY							
THURSDAY							
FRIDAY							

out a chore. It was like a little game; whatever they chose was the chore they had to do for the week. And it would go on the Daily Work Planner Chart.

Now, you see, this relieves you because they don't get mad at you. They've chosen their own chore. They can't say, "Golly, how come I have to do this one again?" They chose it—it was their own fault. So they have to live with it for a week. Notice that Mom and Dad are listed on the chart too. What it shows the kids is that we're working together as a family. At the end of the day, when they've checked their charts and have done their chores as best they can, you can put a little happy face on the chart. Put on a Christmas tree if it's Christmas, or a little Easter cross if it's Easter. Stickers are great also. At the end of the week you can check your chart and say, "You know, our family did a fantastic job this week. We're going to have a picnic at the park, or go bicycling together, or have an evening with popcorn together, or do something else that's fun together because we've really worked well together in accomplishing this. Do you see what that's doing? It's uniting the home and family together.

Setting the Table

Another chore which can be delegated is setting the breakfast table the night before. A five-year-old can learn to set the table. It amazed me when our daughter Jenny would bring her friends home at 16 or 17 years of age and they didn't even know how to set a table. They didn't know where a knife, fork, and spoon went. It wasn't their fault, though. It was because Mom or Dad never took the time to teach them. As the five-year-old sets the table the night before you can say, "Okay, Timmy, do whatever you want. You can use Mom's good china, or you can use paper plates, or you can have candlelight, or you can put your favorite teddy bear on the table. I don't care—whatever you want to do."

One of the things I think about is that too many times we put the good china on the table only for when company comes and at Christmas. Who are the most important people in our life? Our family! And we seldom use the good china for those people who mean the very most to us. I look at it this way: We can't take the china with us, so if a piece gets broken here and there, it gets broken. I would rather have my children be able to enjoy the nicer things and to use them and live with them than to have them in a china cabinet where they can't be enjoyed. So I say let them have the freedom to be able to use their good china, and teach them as you go along.

The Weekly Calendar

Now notice the Weekly Calendar. On this you can list those things which are going to go on for the week. Suzie has to be at the orthodontist, Timmy has football practice, and Bessie has Brownies. You can quickly look through the calendar and see when you're going to be needed, when you're going to need to pick up so and so. And you can feel free now because you know where you're needed and where your children will have to be. You check it over and fill it out the night before so you'll know what's happening the next day. Also fill in your work schedule if you work outside your home. Then your family can see it and know what's going on.

We have to get up early because, even though we have all the modern appliances, we still don't seem to have enough time. Why? Because we're not using them effectively and efficiently. We have to get our homes organized, and for some of us that may mean getting up at five o'clock in the morning. If I were to ask you if you made your bed today, what would you answer? In our seminars about one-third of the women admit to not

WEEKLY CALENDAR

DAY OF WEEK	MONDAY	TUESDAY	WEDNESDAY	THURSDAY	FRIDAY	SATURDAY	SUNDAY
MORNING							
NOON							
NIGHT							

making their bed. How long does it take to make a bed? About two minutes. That's what the average woman says. So what's two minutes out of a whole day to make a bed?

I have a friend who never made her bed. She figures she would just get in it again at night, so why bother to make it? So she never made it. Now she has a son who is 20 years old and is an absolute slob. He's never made his bed because he never had an example. He doesn't know how to put a thing away. He doesn't even know when he pulls out a drawer to push it back in! Nothing is hung up, the bed is never made, and his room is an absolute disaster. It's not really his fault, though, because Mom never took the time to teach him to make his own bed and take care of his room.

The Bed Lesson

I asked our son after his second year in college, "Brad, do you make your bed at school?" He replied, "Mom, I'm the only one in my house who makes his bed." I know why he does it, because once when he was about eight years old he hadn't made his bed for four mornings in a row. I had let him get away with it a little now and then, but four mornings was just too much. He was halfway down the block with a couple of his little buddies when I noticed his unmade bed and went running after him. When I caught up with him I said, "Brad, I really hate to do this, but this is the fourth morning in a row you haven't made your bed. So I'm going to have to ask you to please go back in and make your bed." He replied, "Mom, you wouldn't!" I said, "Well, I'm really sorry, but I'm going to have to do it." He responded, "But I'm going to be late for school!" I came back with, "I know you're going to be late for school, but we'll worry about that later." So he came home and made his bed. Then he said, "You know I'm going to need a note for my teacher." I replied, "Fine, I'll be happy to write you a note." So I wrote him a note saying that Brad was late because this was the fourth morning in a row that he had not made his bed, and that the teacher could do whatever she wanted with him. Do you know what? I never had any trouble with Brad making his bed after that!

I'm not in for a popularity contest to be the number one mom, but I *am* in for being the mom that God wants me to be. Now it was hard for me to do that to Brad. It was as hard for me to call him back into the house as it was for him to actually do it. But over the years it paid off, because it only happened one time. And after that he saw to it that his bed got made.

Also, let them learn to make their own bed. Don't go in and remake it. If you do, they will say, "Why should I even bother. Mom just remakes it anyway." Let them have a crooked bed. As time passes it will become straighter and straighter.

Helping Them Come To Breakfast

After we make the bed we're going to get into the kitchen. (We can get the first load of wash in beforehand if we like.) God tells us several times in the Bible that we can't be lazy as women.

But then we get breakfast cooked and call everyone to the table for breakfast, but they don't come. Isn't that irritating? I think that was one of the things that bothered me the most. So how are we going to correct this problem? I said to the children, "We're going to have a meeting." I continued, "You know I've really got a problem. I call you children for breakfast but you don't come. Now is there anything you might suggest that could help with this problem?" So they said to me, "Golly, Mom, if you'd just let us know a couple of minutes before breakfast is ready, we'd come right to the table." So that's what we did.

You can ring a chime, play the piano, sing a song, blow a whistle, whatever you want to do. Give them a warning to let them know that breakfast or dinner is going to be ready within a few minutes, and they'll come. It absolutely worked beautifully in our family.

Another thing—serve everyone at one time, and don't be a short-order cook. I may be a Christian today, but I'm still Jewish. I want to please everybody because I'm still that good little Jewish mother. So I was fixing French toast for Brad and omelets and pancakes for Jenny. I was fixing oatmeal or whatever they wanted. But what happened to me? I got exhausted. I thought, "This cannot go on." So that's when I came up with the Menu Planner.

The Weekly Menu Planner

I came up with some charts that I called the Weekly Menu Planner. I would have a different breakfast every day, but everyone would eat the same thing every morning. So when Brad came to the table and said, "Ick, I hate oatmeal," I replied to him, "Okay, so you don't like oatmeal. Tomorrow morning, as you see on the Menu Planner, we're going to have French toast, and that's your very favorite." So at least one morning a week we pleased at least one of the children. This worked so beautifully that I decided to extend the idea and make menus for the whole week. Sometimes I even went into two weeks. Also, I tried a new menu at least once a week. (That adds a little variety.)

The Market List

I would make out my menus and then use my Market List. I would check off from the Market List everything I needed at the market that week in order to make out the menu for that week. What happens when

WEEKLY MENU PLANNER

DAY OF WEEK	BREAKFAST	LUNCH	DINNER
MONDAY			
TUESDAY			
WEDNESDAY			
THURSDAY			
FRIDAY			
SATURDAY			
SUNDAY			

MARKET LIST

Qty. Cost

STAPLES

- Flour
- Sugar
- Cereal
- Mixes
- Nuts
- Jell-O
- Stuffing

PASTA

- Spaghetti
- Pasta
- Rice
- Inst. potato
- Mixes

DRINKS

- Coffee
- Tea
- Juice
- Sparkling
- Apple cider

CANNED VEGETABLES

CANNED FRUIT

CONDIMENTS

- Jelly/jam
- Peanut butter
- Honey
- Shortening
- Oil
- Vinegar

CANNED GOODS

- Soups
- Canned meat
- Tuna
- Canned meals

SPICES

- Bacon bits
- Coconut
- Chocolate
- Soda
- Bak. powder
- Salt/pepper

	Qty.	Cost
Syrup		
Molasses		
Catsup		
Mustard		
Mayonnaise		
Salad dressing		
Pickles		
Tomato paste		
Tomato sauce		
Relish		

PAPER GOODS

Paper towels		
Tissues		
Toilet paper		
Napkins		
Glad Wrap		
Waxed paper		
Foil		
Trash bags		
Zip bags-small		
large		

Toothpicks _____

HOUSEHOLD ITEMS

Dishwater soap		
Dish soap		
Clothes soap		
Bleach		
Fab. softener		
Furn. polish		
Light bulbs		
Vacuum bags		

Pet food _____

FRESH PRODUCE

Vegetables		
Fruit		

PERSONAL ITEMS

Makeup		
Toothpaste		
Deodorant		
Hair care		
Body soap		
Fem. protection		

FROZEN FOOD/JUICE

Ice cream		
Vegetables		

DAIRY

Milk
Butter
Cheese
Eggs
Cottage ch.
Sour cream

MEAT

Beef

Chicken

TV dinners

Juice

PASTRY

Crackers
Cookies
Chips
Bread/s
Croutons
Buns

you do this? You don't go to the market and buy things you don't need. You save yourself money and you feel organized inside because you know you have your meals planned. You shop for them and have everything in the house that is going to be in those meals for the week.

Now, let's say Wednesday night comes and your husband calls you up and says, "Honey, I've had a terrible day. I don't even know if I can face anybody, but I want to be with you. Let's go somewhere, just you and I, for dinner." So you look at your Weekly Menu and notice that you had meat loaf planned for that night. What do you do about that? You just move meat loaf over to the next week. Now you have everything in the house and one meal planned for next week. You give your kids waffles or hot dogs or something that night, and you go out with your husband and enjoy your time together. You can be very flexible with your menu planning, especially if you're a working girl. It's so wonderful to know that you have in your mind what needs to be fixed for that night. You almost get excited about going home from work to cook your dinner!

Do you realize that we make an average of 750 meals a year. It's a big area to be organized in. On my own Weekly Calendar, I would do my food shopping on Thursday, so I would always allow enough time on Thursday afternoon to take care of this. When I came home from the market I would then organize my food for all the rest of the week. If you've got several children, and particularly if they're hyperactive children, this is a great way to do it. As you come in from the market you start delegating. One unloads the bags, one folds the bags, one puts away the frozen foods, one puts away the canned goods, and another puts away the dairy products and refrigerator foods. If you have a child who is a little older, you have him or her cleaning all the vegetables.

The Salad Solution

We're big salad and vegetable eaters in our house, so I would buy head lettuce, romaine lettuce, spinach, red leaf lettuce—all the different kinds of lettuce. I would dump them into the kitchen sink, fill it full of water, clean the lettuce carefully, and then set it aside to drain. But you know how it is—all the water never really gets out of the lettuce, so even if you put it in Tupperware, or a baggie, or whatever, the lettuce rusts. So it won't last you as long as you need it to.

So here's how to solve your problem. In the variety section of the supermarket, or at a big drugstore, buy a lingerie bag. (It's a bag with a lot of holes in it.) Now take your lettuce and put it into the lingerie bag. Then put the bag into the washing machine and turn the machine on to the spin cycle. This only takes one or two minutes, so wait right there for the cycle to end. Then you take the lettuce back into the kitchen and tear it up into your Tupperware or baggie. Put it in the refrigerator, and it will last you one to two weeks.

Now what have you done? You've taken a few minutes to make a big tossed green salad. You never have to worry the rest of the week about making a salad. Now take all your vegetables and clean them and cut them up (your broccoli, zucchini, cauliflower, etc.) Put them in Tupperware or a baggie and stick them into the refrigerator, and everything is ready for steamed vegetables, if you have that on your menu for the week. All you have to do is take the vegetables out of the refrigerator and put them in your steamer, and you've got it all done. You'll save yourself hours throughout the week by investing that little bit of time.

I have another solution for you. Should you not want to go to the washing machine to put your lettuce in it, since you feel a little funny about that, buy yourself a team towel and fold it in half. Sew it up on two sides, making a bag out of it, and attach a little bit of ribbon at the side. Now you have a lettuce bag. Put your lettuce in it, and the bag will absorb the water somewhat. Then put it into either your Tupperware or the lettuce compartment in your refrigerator, and you have a cute little lettuce bag. After 24 hours remove the lettuce bag, as it will be soaking wet. This method doesn't do the job as well as spinning it out, but it still does a pretty good job. You can buy a plastic lettuce spinner at your local department store, but why spend more money when you already have a spinner in your service area?

Back to Breakfast

At breakfast time ask each family member, "Where am I going to be needed today? Where do you need me?" Check your Weekly Calendar as you go over the day's plans with them.

Then have everyone take their dishes to the sink. We had a rule in our family that no one ever went to the kitchen empty-handed. Each person always had to pick something up and take it to the sink. I would fill up the sink with hot, sudsy water when I'd get in the kitchen in the morning, and then each person would put all the things into the hot, sudsy water, where it would stay for a little while, until you're ready to get back to it. Now what is this doing? It's saving work for you. It's saving you steps so you have energy to do other things that are more important.

Now we say farewell to our family, because it's time for the children and family to be getting off to school or work. We may even be going to work ourselves, so we really need to have things pulled together and organized. Proverbs 31:26 says, "When she speaks, her words are wise, and kindness is the rule for everything she says," (TLB). What happens is that in the morning, when things are hassled and we're moving around quickly because we've got to get the children ready for school, we can become very irritated. Also, we had to make the bed this morning, and we're not really used to doing that. But at this point we say to our husband, "Honey, is there anything I can do for you today? Is there anything you need me to do for you today?" Maybe you need to go to the hardware store for him or whatever. He'll fall over in a dead faint the first morning you ask him, but then he will probably come up with a nice list of things the next day.

Then quickly check each child's room with him or her. Also quickly check the bathrooms, and have the children wipe the toothpaste off the mirror. Once or twice a week you might want to go in and do a really good job, but get them used to cleaning up after themselves so they won't think you're a little maid who will go around every day cleaning up after them. Then, as they're leaving the house, check to see if they have their lunch, their lunch money, their books, their homework, their gym clothes, their reports, or whatever they need.

One thing that bothered me a lot was that just when I really got into my housework the phone would ring and one of the kids would say, "Oh, I forgot such-and-such. Would you bring it to school?" So you drive to their school and you look all over campus for your child who forgot something. And you've lost an hour of your day before you know it. So take those few minutes to check with the kids in the morning, before they leave the house, to see that they have everything they need.

Say Something Good

When your kids have done something well, be sure to compliment them on it. I teach a Friday morning Bible study in my home, and one day I thought I would throw out this suggestion to the girls: Write down six items that you like about yourself. You wouldn't believe how hard this was for them. They were hemming and hawing around. They couldn't figure out anything to write down. You see, what happens over the years is that we've had parents, plus brothers and sisters, plus teachers who have repeatedly put us down. So as we've grown up we've developed bad self-esteem.

Therefore we need to compliment our children when they do something well. "Timmy, you did such a neat job setting the table this morning. I just love the way you put your teddy bear on the table." You know what's going to happen tomorrow morning? He won't be able to wait to show what else he's done for you, and he'll become eager to do these chores. "Susie, I'm so pleased with you today—you got your shoes on the right feet, and your socks match. Thank you so much for working on that." As you begin to compliment them and build into them a good self-esteem, and as you send them off with a loving hug, you help them to remember you as a smiling mother and not as a screaming shrew.

God says in Proverbs 31:17, that the virtuous woman is energetic and a hard worker. So we gals can't fall back into bed, can we? Besides, the bed is made, so it's not quite so tempting to get back into it! We have to keep going, to get the second load of wash in, to get the dishes done. Now we can check our Menu Planner to see what we're going to have for dinner tonight, to see that we've taken what we need to out of the freezer. Remember, we have all those things in the house already, so we feel free and comfortable about our meals for the day. Then we get our counters cleaned up and water our house plants, and we rejoice that our basic housework is done at only 9:00 in the morning.

The Right Priorities

God tells us in Proverbs 31:27-30, "She watches carefully all that goes on throughout her household, and is never lazy. Her children stand and bless her; so does her husband. He praises her with these words: There are many fine women in the world, but you are the best of them all!" (TLB).

How do we receive that kind of praise from our children and our husband? There's only one way that I know of that will cause them to give us that genuine kind of praise, and that's by having our priorities as a Christian woman in order.

Do you know what our priorities are? God tells us in Matthew 6:33, "Seek ye first the kingdom of God and His righteousness, and all these things will be added unto you." Our number one priority is God. There have been times in my life when I got my priorities out of order. There was a time when I needed to have a special time with my Lord, but the only time available was at 5:00 in the morning, when the house was still. And that was hard, because I might have been up three times during the night with the children. But I got up and spent that little time. I committed my works to the Lord, and my plans were established (Proverbs 16:3). On some days, I would check my calendar and say, "There's no way I'm going to get everything done that I have to do today." But then I would get up early in the morning, share a little in God's Word, put my hands on the calendar, and say, "Lord, You know what I have to do today. Would You help me and guide me through every moment of the day? Show me what You will have me to do." Do you know what happened on the days I did that? I got everything done and had time for a nap in the afternoon.

The Other Priorities

Our second priority is our husband. Our third priority is our children. Our fourth priority is our home. And number five is all the other things. That means helping a philanthropic group, being a Brownie leader, leading a Bible study, having luncheons out with the ladies, shopping, and all those things. I'll never forget the day my husband came to me and said, "Emilie, you love those children more than you do me." Well, I had to take care of the children. I said, "They need me. I have to do all these things for them." But in my heart I knew he was right. I knew he was being neglected because he was telling me he didn't feel that he had a priority in my life over the children.

We women often get our priorities mixed up. I still struggle with it. Sometimes the number one priority, which is God, becomes number six or seven on the list. Husband can be eight or nine. Children can be number one, and all the other things we do number two. We're good at that. But, God tells us that our children will stand and bless us, and so will our husbands, as long as we get our priorities in order. So remember that God is there. He's given those children to you as a gift. He's going to take care of them for you. Keep them in the right priority. Remember that you were a wife to your husband before you were a mother to your children.

Someday, and it won't be long, those children are going to be out of the nest. They're going to be creating homes and families of their own and will be going off to college and off to work. And then you and your husband will be alone in that home. If you haven't worked on developing a relationship and spending time together and making him an important priority in your life, at that point you'll look at each other and either love and know and communicate with each other, or else simply be two strangers looking at each other.

If you're working outside the home and have your priorities out of order, I recommend to you that you stop working until you get those priorities in order. You say, "But I have to work." I had a gal come up to me after a class and say, "Boy, I didn't like what you said. I was working and I loved my job." (Her husband was an unbeliever and she was having trouble in her marriage.) She continued, "That job was so important to me, but my house was all out of order. That's why I came to the organization class. I just rejected everything you said. After two weeks, things got even worse in my home, and I began thinking. God began to work in my heart. He said, 'You better get your home in order.' So I decided that I was going to quit my job and work on my priorities and get my home organized and in order. So I went to my husband and said to him, 'Honey, I'm going to quit my job.' He replied, 'Who's going to pay the car payment?' I said, 'Sell the car.' He responded, 'Well, okay.' So I quit my job."

Later she said to me, "I got my home in order. I got all the things done that I needed to do. Now my relationship with my husband is getting better. Soon we're going to have a Valentine party at our church."

She continued, "He had never before set a foot into our church, but I thought I would invite him one more time. I said, 'We're having a Valentine dinner at church; would you like to go with me?' He replied, 'Yes, I would.' If I had planned that evening myself, it couldn't have been better. Later my husband said to me, 'Let me know anytime you have something at church that's special. I'd like to go with you.'"

So, you see, when you get your priorities in order, God will take care of the rest.

Evening Time

Now its evening time. We get a fire lit and some candles going. We may prepare a few little munchies. (Remember, we've got everything all prepared. All the vegetables are cut and cleaned in the refrigerator.) We can make a little sour cream, cottage cheese, garlic salt, and lemon juice dip. If the kids get a little wild, we can just throw a sheet on the floor, give them some veggies and a little dip, and let them have a little fun.

You know, that five o'clock hour was a terrible time. They were tired of you and you were certainly tired of them by then. So you may need to prepare yourself a bit. Freshen up your makeup. (Remember, it was six o'clock in the morning when you first did that.) Put on a little perfume and smell good. And then start thinking toward a quiet and gentle spirit. How can you possibly do that? Well, God tells us that we are to start thinking of a quiet and gentle spirit.

But right now it's five o'clock and a zoo around the house. There's spilled milk all over the kitchen floor, and something's boiling over on the stove. The dog and cat are hungry and nipping at your heels. You've got kids all around you. Then the phone rings. And you're supposed to have a quiet and gentle spirit? It's tough, isn't it?

Did you know what I did at times like this? I just went into the bathroom, closed the door, and put my head in the potty. I said, "Lord, You said that I need a quiet and gentle spirit. So I'm asking for it." Then I went back out, and you know what? I didn't get it. So I went back into the bathroom again and said, "You know, God, I didn't get it. You don't know what it's like out there." I might have had to go back and forth two or three times. But eventually my heart was quieted and I was able to pull the kids together and organize them as best as I could.

Then I would be ready for my husband's arrival. When I heard his car coming up the driveway, or him walking up the driveway, I would drop everything and go to greet him. Now I know you're diapering that baby, but throw a diaper over him and go and greet your husband. What does it tell him when you run to the door to greet him as he comes in from work? You're telling him that he's important to you. He's first place. You don't know how long he's been on the freeway driving it out. You don't know what happened at work today—whether he had to fire his best friend, or the construction job fell under. You do not know what went on that whole day.

That husband of yours could have gone a hundred different places that night. There are tons of women out there who would like your husband. I don't care what he looks like or what kind of shape he's in. They'd like him. But he has chosen to come home to you. He's coming through that door to you. So take those few minutes. Go to the door, greet him, throw your arms around him. Tell him that you're happy he's home, that you're thankful he's worked hard all day and provided for this home, for you and your children. Then let him have a few minutes to unwind with the paper or the mail or whatever. Try not to share the negative parts of the day with him until after dinner.

Then enjoy your family. God has given that family to you as a gift. If we're raising little wild Indians, they're not fun to enjoy, are they? Maybe only Mom and Dad can put up with them. But other people don't want to be around them. So lovingly discipline them. Teach them obedience and responsibility. They're a very precious legacy that God has given to you. They grow up very quickly, and they will grow up to be beautiful children if you lovingly discipline them.

On the following pages you will find an example of

charts you can make into a notebook to better organize these areas of daily life:

The Expenditures Chart

Ecclesiastes 3:1 NIV says, "There is a time for everything, and a season for every activity under heaven"—and that means even organization. On the Expenditures Chart, each month you can list your house payment or rent, your food, your utilities, your babysitting expenses, your insurance, your telephone, your clothing, your beauty parlor, your taxes, and your donations. Then at the end of the year you'll have the totals for all the expenses you've had during the year, and this will be very easy to take to your tax person.

The Family History Chart

The next section is your Family History Chart. Here you can list your children's names, their birth dates, their bloods types, their yearly physical, their dental exams, their eye exam, when they had their innoculations, etc. Everything is nicely listed here so you can refer back to it.

The Credit Card Sheet

The next section is your Credit Card Information Sheet. You should list the name of the company, the address, the telephone number, and when the card expires. Then, if it's lost or stolen, you can quickly go to your notebook and report it immediately. If you do some purchasing over the telephone, you have the number handy, and you won't have to fumble through your purse trying to find your credit card.

The Emergency Sheet

Then there's the Emergency Sheet. List the police, the fire department, the ambulance service, the poison control service, the neighbor, etc. One gal said to me, "I started making out my notebook when I came to this

'Who to Call if Sheet. So I started listing all the telephone numbers. Then I noticed the Poison Control heading. Well, I hadn't even known that there was such a thing! So I looked through the phone book, but I couldn't find the number. I called the information operator, but she didn't know too much about it either. It took me several minutes to finally get the number of the poison control. So that listing on the chart could have saved a child's life. If my child had taken something and I had to try to find the number, it could have been four or five minutes before I could have found it."

Dates and Occasions

Then you have Dates and Occasions To Remember. List everybody's birthday, everybody's anniversary, and all the other important dates for the year. As each month comes up, check to see whose birthday it is. You can show on the chart if you sent them a card or what kind of gift you gave them last year.

The Home Instruction Sheet

Then a Home Instruction Sheet comes next. If you should go away on vacation, or someone should come into your home to take care of your children, they can see what time Sunday school starts, where the church is, any appointments you may have during the week, and when the trash is picked up. Maybe your mother-in-law sees this man walking around in your backyard one day, and she doesn't know who he is. She can check the home instruction sheet and say, "That's the pool man, or that's the gardener, so I'm not going to worry about him."

The Entertainment Sheet

Then there's an Entertainment Sheet. This is excellent because if you're going to have a party or a buffet or whatever, you can list the guests, the time and date, what type of party, if you're going to have a theme, your menu, your table decoration, etc. You can also write down any notes that you might want to make after the evening is over.

Tips on Taxes

Purchase a dozen 5" x 10" envelopes. These are for all your receipts and check stubs, one for each month of the year. Insert all your receipts and check stubs in the envelope. Then take these envelopes plus your expenditures sheet to your tax man and everything is in order to make out your tax return.

FAMILY HOUSEHOLD EXPENDITURES

Month of _____

House Payment/ Rent	Food	Utilities	Furniture/ Repairs	Car/ Gas	Insurance	Phone	Clothing	Clothing/ House Clean	Haircuts	School Expenses

Credit Card Charges	Investments	DEDUCTIBLE ITEMS						
		Medical/ Dental	Medicines	Baby-sitting	Taxes	Donations	Savings	Other Misc. Expenses

FAMILY HISTORY

Family Member Name	Birth Date	Blood Type	Date of Last:				Inoculation/ Date	Other
			Yearly Physical	Dental Exam	Eye Exam			

Family Member Name	SIZES					Favorite Activities	Other Clubs, Interests, Etc.
	Dress/Suit	Shoes	Pants	Socks	Underwear		

OUR CREDIT CARDS

If lost or stolen, notify company at once.

Company	Card Number	Company Address	Company Phone Number	Card Expires (Date)

WHO TO CALL IF . . .

Service Person	Phone Number	Service Person	Phone Number
POLICE		GAS CO. EMERGENCY	
FIRE		NEWSPAPER	
AMBULANCE		INSURANCE (HOME)	
POISON CONTROL		INSURANCE (CAR)	
DOCTOR		APPLIANCE REPAIR	
DENTIST		PLUMBER	
ORTHODONTIST		ELECTRICIAN	
SCHOOL(S)		GLASS REPAIR	
SCHOOL(S)		VET	
NEIGHBOR		CAT'S NAME	
PASTOR		DOG'S NAME	
HUSBAND'S WORK NO.		POOL SERVICE	
HEATING/AIR COND. REPAIR PERSON		GARDENER	

DATES AND OCCASIONS
TO REMEMBER

Month	Date/Occasion	Name of Person(s)	Gift(s) Given
JANUARY			
FEBRUARY			
MARCH			
APRIL			
MAY			
JUNE			

HOME INSTRUCTIONS

Day of Week	Routine Chores/ Errands	Special Appointments
SUNDAY		
MONDAY		
TUESDAY		
WEDNESDAY		
THURSDAY		
FRIDAY		
SATURDAY		

ENTERTAINMENT

Date _____

Guests	Time/Date	Dinner/Party Type	Menu	Decorations/ Centerpiece/ Tablecloth

Games/ Entertainment	Dress	Help: Hired/ Voluntary	Notes

3

TOTAL MESS TO TOTAL REST

Suppose I were to say to you, "Today I'm going to come home with you. I want you to take me into your house, and I want to go through your closets, to look under your bed, to open your drawers, to look in your pantry, and to go anyplace in your house. I just want to check out your house really good."

Some of you would reply, "Well, that's okay. I've got my house in order, and things are really good there, so you can come over." Others of you would say, "Okay, but don't go into the third bedroom, because I've been shoving things in that back bedroom for a long time. That's my little hideaway. You can't go back there, but you can look everywhere else." Still others of you might say, "There is no way anybody is going to come into my house, because the whole place is a total mess."

Controlling Your Home

Now we're going to show you how to take that mess, no matter what size it is, and turn it into a home that you'll be able to maintain and be able to rest in. You will control your home instead of your home controlling you.

Here's some of the equipment you'll need in order to work out this program. You'll also need three to ten boxes with lids 16" deep by 12" wide by 10" high. You'll need a 3" x 5" card-file box and some 3" x 5" card files. I like to use the colored files because sometimes it's easier to remember the color than what you've written on the tab. Get ten cards in each color—blue, yellow, white, green, orange, cherry. Be sure to get some little tabs for each section of cards, and also a pen to write on them. Then you'll need at least ten colored file folders. (I like to use the colored ones because they help to identify things.) If you already have a metal file cabinet at home, that's great, but most people don't have one. The file boxes are a lot less expensive.

I've been teaching my seminars for several years now, and after about the first six months I discovered something about us women. Our intentions are good and we want to get started, but somehow we can't seem to get organized enough to get ourselves organized, and we just throw the whole program out the window. So pray about the program. Ask God to make you willing to get the materials and to incorporate them into your home.

Commit Yourself

You'll want to commit yourself to five weeks in taking that total mess and cleaning it up. I don't want you to become overwhelmed thinking about it, because you're going to take a small portion at a time—only one room a week for the next five weeks. You'll do it nice and slow, so that you'll gradually get your home under control.

Now we're going to take three large boxes, or, if you prefer, three large trash bags. I like the trash bags because they're lightweight and you can drag them through the house. So take your three trash bags and label one of them "Put Away," one "Throw Away," and one "Give Away."

Now visualize yourself standing at the front door with these three big trash bags. Ring the door bell, then walk through the front door. The first room you come to will be the first room you're going to clean, with the exception of the kitchen. (If that's the room you walk into first, you'll save the kitchen till the fifth week, because you'll need all the experience you can get by the time you get to the kitchen.) To make it easy, let's say we step into the living room, and on our right is the hall closet.

So we open up the hall closet. We're now going to take everything out of that hall closet. We have to make a decision, and that is to get kind of vicious in making choices about what to do with all the stuff we've taken out of the hall closet. I recommend that you call on a friend who would like to help you with your house (and you with her house). It's great to have a friend because she'll help you make decisions that you haven't been able to make for 15 years. She'll tell you, "Throw it out or give it away," and that will be very helpful to you.

The Hall Closet

Now, we're going to put into the hall closet all those things which actually belong in a hall closet. These include sweaters, coats, umbrella, boots, football blanket, binoculars, tennis racket, etc.

But now we have all these other things that don't belong in there, such as old magazines that we've collected for six or seven years. (We are going to look through them some rainy day and cut out the pictures and recipes, but we never did). So we have to get rid of these things. We've also got papers and receipts and all sorts of other things in that hall closet, so we'll put these either in the Put Away bag, the Throw Away bag, or the Give Away bag.

As we go through our home every week, for the next five weeks, we begin to fill up these bags. At the end of the fifth week we may have three, ten or fifteen bags full of various things. Then we put twisties on the trash bags marked Throw Away and set them out for the trash man. Now they're gone! You've got all those things out of the way.

So now you have two bags left, the Give Away bag and the Put Away bag. The Give Away bag will hold things that maybe you want to hand down to some other family member or to relatives. Or it might include clothing that you want to give to a thrift shop or sell at a rummage sale or donate to your church.

Maybe you want to co-op—three or four of you who have done the five-week program may want to have a garage sale and make a little extra money. Buy something for yourself or for the house, or give it to your church or missionary group or whatever. So you've cleaned these things out of your house and put them to good use in somebody else's hands.

Keeping It Neat

Now we have our house totally clean. So how are we going to maintain it that way? We certainly never want to go through this total mess again! The cleanup was enough to do for five weeks, and we don't *have* to do it again.

The way in which we maintain our house now is to take our 3" x 5" cards and label each of the tabs. The first color is going to be labeled "Daily." On these cards we list all those things that we have to do daily in our house in order to maintain it, such as washing the dishes and making the bed (plus all the other daily things).

The second section is those things we do weekly. For example, on Monday we wash; on Tuesday we iron and water the house plants; on Wednesday we mop the floors; on Thursday we vacuum and do our marketing; and so on through the week.

So now Thursday comes along, and Sue, your very special friend, calls you and says, "Let's go to lunch and go shopping. The department store has a big sale today." So you check your cards and say, "I've done all my daily things, but it's Thursday, so I have to vacuum and go to the market. I can do my marketing this afternoon when we get back from lunch, but I don't know about the vacuuming."

So you go with Sue and get your bargains, but the vacuuming isn't done. So you decide to move the vacuuming over to Friday. But you look on Friday's card and see all those other things to do on Friday. So you take Friday's chores and move them to Saturday. But on Saturday you're going to the park with the kids. So you decide to move those things to *Sunday* now. But on Sunday you can't do them either because you're going to church and you've also got company coming afterwards. So here we are going around in circles again. We've moved one job from day to day, but we're completely confused.

So we don't do that. Instead, on Thursday, when we go to lunch with Sue and don't have time to vacuum, we move our vacuuming card to the back of the file. This means we don't vacuum our house again until next Thursday, when the vacuuming card comes up in our file again. In other words, we rotate our cards daily whether we do the allotted jobs or not.

This means that we're crunching along on dirty carpet for a week or two. You say, "I can't possibly do that." But now you're disciplining yourself to keep your priorities in order. So next week, when Sue calls and says, "Let's go to lunch," you'll tell her, "I'll go to lunch if I get my vacuuming done, because if I don't get it done

today it means another whole week before I can do it."
Remember, *you* want to be in control of your home, and
not the other way around.

Next you have your monthly things. During week 1
you clean the refrigerator: (you have a whole week to do
it, or you can delegate the job to a child). During week 2
you do the oven, and so forth. This way, every week
you're doing a little bit to maintain your home. It's only
going to take you a little time, but you're continually
maintaining your home so you never have to go through
that total mess program again. Next you have your
quarterly things to do (straighten drawers, etc.). Then
you have you biannual things to do (rearrange furniture, wash curtains, etc.) Finally there are the annual
things, such as cleaning the basement, attic, garage,
etc.

Your last tab, at the very back of your file, is your
storage tab. Here you take your 3″ x 5″ card files and
number them Box 1, Box 2, Box 3 and so forth. Then you
take your storage boxes that you've been collecting (or
that you've purchased), line them all up, and number
them Box 1, Box 2, Box 3, etc. You've got all these boxes
in a row now, and a card that corresponds with each
box.

If you want to go a step further, you can make out *two*
cards for each box, one to be pasted on the box and one
to go into your card file. Remember that Put Away bag,
with Billy's first baby blanket, etc.? Well, you put all
these things into Box 1. Then you list on the 3″ x 5″ card
labeled Box 1 all the things which are actually in the
box. And you do that with all the things you find in those
Put Away bags.

Maintaining Memories

Not long ago our son Brad came home from college
and said to Dad, "Remember when you used to referee

those football and basketball games, and you wore that black-and-white striped shirt? Well, I'd like to wear it because we're going to have a black-and-white party at school and you can't get into this party unless you wear black and white. So I'd like to wear your shirt."

Bob kind of looked at me and thought to himself, "I don't know where the shirt is. I haven't seen the shirt for 15 years." But I knew where the shirt was. I went right over to my card file, checked it out, and said, "Oh, yes, it's Box 5." So I said to Brad and Bob, "Go out into the garage, look up on the shelf, find Box 5, pull it down, and inside that box you will find your black-and-white referee shirt." Sure enough, there it was, and Brad wore the shirt to the party!

Now as we take our file box and our colored file folders and look in that Put Away bag, what do we find? We find old newspaper clippings, warranties, instruction booklets, receipts from car repairs and household repairs, and all kinds of other things. So we take our colored file folders, list all those things, and file the cards away in our file box.

Receipts Equal Money

Not long ago I had a neat experience. The icemaker on our refrigerator broke for the second time. When I called the repairman he said, "Mrs. Barnes, that's the same thing I fixed about six months ago." I asked, "How much will it cost?" He replied, "Sixty-five dollars. However, it's under warranty, if you can find the receipt."

Well, little did he know! I went right to my file, looked under Repair Receipts, and within 30 seconds had the receipt. I asked him, "Is this what you need?" He replied, "Yes, you've just saved yourself 65 dollars."

The Children's File Box

When our children were about 12 or 13 years old, I set

up a file box for them. (I wish I had done it even earlier). I gave them ten file folders, and one day we went through the Total Mess program in their rooms. So they began to file all their report cards, all their special reports, and all their pictures and letters. Jenny was lucky enough to get some love letters, so she filed those in her file box. She also pressed and filed the flowers from her special dates and proms. When she got her first car, the insurance papers all went into the file box.

When the children went away to college, the first thing they took with them was their file box, because it had all their important papers. When they came home for the summer, home came the file box. When Jenny and Craig were married in September, she took her file box with her. All her little treasures were in that box. Then she got another box and ten more file folders, and she set up a household file box. So now she has all those warranties, instruction booklets, and insurance papers in her household file.

So what have we done? We've taken that total mess and changed it into total rest. And we'll maintain that rest. What does that give us? More hours in our day, with no guilt feelings about an unorganized house.

Total Mess to Total Rest Chart

EQUIPMENT NEEDED

3 to 10 boxes with lids (tops)
3" x 5" card file
3" x 5" colored cards with dividers w/colored tags.
File box and file folders

HOW TO GET ORGANIZED

A. Begin by collecting boxes with lids (tops).
B. Plan a 5-week program project.

C. Label 3 larges boxes or trash bags as follows:
1. Put Away
2. Throw Away
3. Give Away
D. Start at your front door and go through your house, starting with the living room and ending with the kitchen.
1. Closets, drawers, shelves.
2. Get vicious!!

HOUSEHOLD ROUTINE

A. Set up a 3″ x 5″ colored card file with dividers.
B. Label dividers in this card file as follows:
1. Daily   5. Biannual
2. Weekly   6. Annual
3. Monthly   7. Storage
4. Quarterly
C. Make a list of jobs:
1. Daily:
   a. dishes
   b. make beds
   c. clean bathrooms
   d. pick up rooms
   e. pick up kitchen
2. Weekly:
   a. Monday—wash, marketing
   b. Tuesday—iron, water plants
   c. Wednesday—mop floors
   d. Thursday—vacuum, shopping
   e. Friday—change bed linens
   f. Saturday—yardwork
   g. Sunday—free except to plan for next week.
NOTE: If you skip a job on an allotted day, DON'T DO IT—SKIP IT UNTIL NEXT WEEK AND PUT CARD BEHIND FILE.

3. Monthly:
   a. Week #1—Clean refrigerator
   b. Week #2—Clean oven
   c. Week #3—Mending
   d. Week #4—Clean and dust baseboards

4. Quarterly:
   a. Drawers, windows
   b. Closets, move furniture and vacuum
   c. China cabinets, cupboards

   Ask yourself, "How clean does my house have to be to keep my family happy?"

5. Biannual:
   a. Screens
   b. Rearrange furniture

6. Annual:
   a. Wash curtains
   b. Clean drapes
   c. Clean carpets
   d. Wash walls

STORAGE

A. Get boxes with tops and number each box.
B. Assign each box a 3 x 5 card w/corresponding number. For example:
   Box #1—a. Bill's baby clothes
            b. Bill's baby book
   Box #2—Toys
   Box #3—Seasonal clothes
   Box #4—Christmas decorations
   Box #5—Books: high school yearbooks, materials
   Box #6—Scrapbooks

Box #7—Old pictures
Box #8—Snow clothes
Box #9—Scrap fabrics

C. File box with file folders—label as follows:
  1. Report cards
  2. Appliance instructions
  3. Warranties
  4. Decorating ideas
  5. Insurance papers and booklets
  6. Special notes, letters, cards
  7. Car repair receipts
  8. Receipts from purchases such as furniture/
     antiques

4

PURSE ORGANIZATION

Pete has just returned with the baby-sitter and you're running late for that long-looked-forward-to class reunion. But you want everything to be perfect.

Julie has spilled the cat's milk dish and you're sticking to the kitchen floor, trying to clean up the milk. The phone rings and the rollers are falling out of your hair. "Time, I need more time!" You're crying. Pete takes over the mess. Your sitter holds baby Jason and you put Julie in her rocker with a book. Now it's time for you. You're hurrying to get ready and be out of the house on time. Grabbing your cute color-matching clutch pocketbook, you begin to change purses. As you try to decide what to take out of your everyday bag with papers, gum wrappers, pacifiers, etc. rolling around the bottom, you begin to get upset and frustrated. Dumping the whole contents of the purse on the bed, you throw up your hands and say "forget it!" You may even end up taking your crummy tote bag that doesn't match or coordinate at all with your lovely outfit.

However, if you keep a well-organized purse, it will

be ever so simple to change bags and do it quickly. You will never need to hassle with your purse-changing again.

Getting Started

What you'll need is a nice-size purse for everyday use plus three to seven little purses. They can be made of quilted fabric (with zipper or Velcro fasteners) or of denim or corduroy prints (make each little purse different in color and size to identify it more easily.) Your everyday handbag should be pretty good-sized, since it's the one you'll be dragging around with you (and your kids) in and out of the market and all over the place. It should have everything in it that you'll need. This is practically your whole life now in your handbag.

The Wallet

First we'll need to find a wallet that's functional for you. A wallet is very, very important. You want a wallet that has a little section where you can keep a few bills. Then it should have a zipper compartment where you can keep some change. (You should also keep a pen with your wallet.) Keep your credit cards which you frequently use in your wallet, and also your checkbook, your driver's license, and all those other little important things. So now when you run to the cleaner or the pharmacy to pick something up, rather than taking your big purse with everything in it, all you have to do is pull your wallet out of your purse, run in, and make your little exchange. Then you put the wallet back into your purse.

The Little Bags

In the little bags you'll keep all sorts of things. In my little makeup bag I keep such things as a mirror, lipstick, lipliner, lipgloss, spot remover, perfume, blush, nail clippers, nail file, etc. I also keep some change for an emergency phone call.

In addition to my wallet, sunglasses bag, and makeup bag, I keep in my purse another little makeup bag, a bag for reading glasses, and two more small bags for various items. The contents of all these bags are described on the chart labeled "Purse Organization Chart."

Everything Organized

Remember the day that Sue called you and said she wanted to go out to lunch with you? Well, now if you decide to go to lunch, you just grab your clutch purse and put a few of the little bags in it. For example, you'll want to take your wallet and credit cards plus your makeup bags. How long will this take you? Not even a minute. You just stick your purse under your arm, and you're off for the day. And when you come home again, you just take out the things and put them back into your everyday purse.

Odds and Ends

Now we need to take care of the odds and ends throughout our home to help us to be organized. Once or twice a year I go to a card shop where they have all kinds of greeting cards—birthday cards, anniversary cards, sympathy cards, etc. Rather than running out 15 or 20 times during the year, I spend 30 minutes to an hour once or twice a year at a card shop. I take the sheet labeled "Dates and Occasions to Remember" to help me pick out the cards for everyone that I'm going to need to send a card to throughout the year. Along with that I'll add some anniversary cards, some get-well cards, and some sympathy cards. (I need a few of those on hand.) Then I file all the cards in file folders marked "Greeting Cards."

The Gift Shelf

Somewhere in your home it's nice to have a gift shelf.

At any of the department stores that have sales, pick up
a few nice items. A little box of stationery, or little teddy
bears, or whatever is on sale should go on your shelf. I've
always had a little gift shelf in my home, so when the
children have a birthday party they have to go to, I
would let them go to the shelf and pick out what they
wanted to give to Scotty or Lori or whomever. This way
you've got something right there all the time, so you're
not running out to a department store spending a lot of
time and money. Where it's only costing you two or
three dollars this way, you might have spent ten of fifteen dollars because you were in a hurry and didn't have
the time to find bargains. So have a little area in your
home where you can have some toys and books and
other little gift items all ready to go.

The Gift Wrap Shelf

Then I also like to have a gift wrap shelf (or box or
drawer). Once a year I'll go to where they have gift
wrap on sale. (We have several places in our area, and
you may also.) Once a year I buy all my Christmas wrap
plus straw flowers and everything I need to wrap
packages. One year I had red-and-white polka dot
paper for Christmas, but that didn't stop me. Anytime
during the year I could put a red ribbon on it, a white
ribbon on it, a blue ribbon on it, or a yellow ribbon on it.
And I had that same wrap for any occasion throughout
the year. So I always had something with which I could
wrap a package right away.

In that little gift wrap section you should have some
colored ribbon, some Scotch tape, and a few straw
flowers to put on a package. Another cute thing is to go
out to the yard and pick a little creeping Charlie and
stick it on a package (or a few little chrysanthemums, or
daisies or other fresh flowers). Then you should also
have some brown paper for mailing packages, along

with some mailing labels, some string, and some strapping tape.

The Home Office

Somewhere in your home you should have a home office. This is wonderful to have, perhaps in the kitchen, a bedroom, or even the garage. In this office should be a desk, some shelves, scissors, paper clips, pens, pencils, Scotch tape, thank you notes, marking pens, postcards, and stamp. (I hate to stand in line at the post office. Every time I go the line seems to get longer. So I go once or twice a year. I buy a nice big fat roll of stamps that cost a lot of money, but I figure it's worth it.)

Also have a glue stick, a rubber stamp pad, and a rubber stamp. When our children were about 15 years old, I gave them in their Christmas stocking one year a rubber stamp pad and a little rubber stamp made with their name, address, and telephone number. They could use this on their school papers or for a return address on the little cards and thank you notes that they send out. Now you don't give this to a five-year-old because if you do, he'll be stamping his name all over the wallpaper and everywhere else. So use your head on this. But kids love those little rubber stamps, and they make super gifts.

Then get some stationery, a letter opener, a memo pad, a paperweight, some string, a dictionary, and a file box with your colored file folders. You already have these in your five-week program, so this is no extra trouble.

Telephone Items

What do you actually keep next to your telephone? One of the things I dislike is to make a telephone book. Every so many years (or months) you have to redo the address book, and I just hate that because it takes a lot of time. Well, I found this handy little telephone address file that has the separate little cards that can be pulled out. One brand is called a Rolodex Card File. With this system you fill out a separate card for each person, and then if there's a change you can either erase the information or fill out a new card. This way you just change the cards gradually as time goes on instead of rewriting a whole book once a year.

Also by your telephone you should have some pens and pencils, some scissors, a letter opener, a memo pad, and a calling card file. A calling card file is a little packet that has plastic pages inside in which you can insert business cards. Remember that Put Away Bag that now has those business cards from drawers and all over the place? Well, now you have a place to put them—in this nice little packet. This can go in a drawer by the telephone, and it makes a great gift for Father's Day. It's nice for a stocking stuffer at Christmas, too.

Also by your telephone you should have your emergency telephone numbers. (See the sheet covering this described earlier in this book.)

Your Own Business Card

You should consider the possibility of having your own business card. I know you're saying, "But I'm just a mom; I don't need a business card or calling card." My sister-in-law gave me some calling cards when our children were little. They had my name, telephone number, and then all around the card they had all the little fun things that I like to do. As it turned out, I couldn't believe how much I used those cards. I'd see a mother at school who would tell me her son was going to come home with my son to play, so could she have my phone number and address. Instead of fumbling through my purse finding a pen and piece of paper, all I did was zip out my little business card and hand it to her. She would look at it and say, "Golly, that's neat. I didn't know you knew how to make homemade bread," or "I didn't know you taught a time management class."

Things in Your Car

Then consider the things you keep in your automobile, in your glove compartment or your trunk. These are things, too, that will help to keep you at ease. You should have a flashlight, some maps, a can opener, some change for emergency telephone calls, some reading material, some business cards, a few Band-Aids, some matches, some stationery, some pens and pencils, a blanket, a towel, and scissors.

In the trunk you should have a few fuses, a rope, a jumper cable, some flares, and a first aid kit. Somewhere you should have a Hide-a-Key. If you ever lock yourself out of your car, you'll wish you had a magnetic Hide-a-Key box stuck somewhere under a fender or bumper of your car.

Purse Organization

Purse size to fit your frame—not too small and not too large!

What goes in your purse:

A. Wallet:

money/checkbook	driver's license
change compartment	calendar (current)
pen/credit cards	pictures (most used)

B. Makeup Bag #1:

lipstick	mirror
comb/small brush	dime
blush	

C. Makeup Bag #2:

nail file	scissors (small)

small perfume
hand cream
nail clippers

kleenex tissues
breath mints/gum/
cough drops
matches

D. Eyeglass case for sunglasses.

E. Eyeglass case for reading/spare glasses.

F. Small Bag—Etc. Bag #1:
   business cards (yours & your husband's)
   —hair dresser
   —insuranceman
   —auto club
   —doctor (health plan)
   library card
   seldom-used credit cards
   small calculator
   tea bag/Sweet 'n Low/Aspirin

G. Small Bag—Etc. Bag #2:
   reading materials
   —small Bible/paperback book
   toothbrush
   Wash 'n Dry
   needle/thread/pins/thimble
   Band-Aid
   toothpicks
   collapsible cup
   Basic H cleaner
   tape measure
   feminine protection

Each of these bags can be made of different materials to make locating items much easier.

5

CREATIVE ENTERTAINING

Something I discovered not too many years ago was the idea of using sheets as tablecloths and napkins. One of the things that's great about using sheets is that you get lots of fabric for a modest amount of money, plus they're all wash-and-wear. You can wash them, throw them into the dryer, and put them right back onto the table. So throw away the plastic cloth you've wiped off for years, and get into sheets!

If you're going to be married or want to buy a new set of dishes, you might want to buy just a plain set of white dishes or bone dishes. They will go with anything you choose, any kind of tablecloth or anything else you choose. But we can't all go out and do that, so we may have to do with what we have. My everyday dishes happen to be brown-and-white calico dishes. So I started looking for sheets that would go with my brown-and-white dishes, and I had a lot of fun doing this. One set I bought in the basement of a department store. It has a little border on the bottom and some black and white and brown on the top.

Using What We Have

So now you say, "Well, Emilie, you've got a border on the bottom of the sheet. Don't you cut off the border? You only have one border on a sheet." No, I don't cut off the border. I place the sheet so that the border shows on the most obvious end of the table. This way, as you walk into my dining room or family room you see the sheet on the table with the border showing. Nobody has ever come into my home and run around to the other side of the table to see if there's a border over there.

I took the bottom sheet (the fitted sheet), which happened to be a print, and made napkins out of it. Then for a napkin holder I used a little star-shaped cookie cutter. With some white daisies on the table, I have a pretty little table setting at very low cost.

Or for a napkin holder you might try using one of those big fat paper clips that you can buy in a stationery store. They come in all different bright colors, and they make great little gifts.

Placemats

Placemats are another nice thing to have. You can make them out of quilted fabric. A yard-and-a-half of fabric will make four placemats. Double up the quilted fabric and put the two right sides together . Cut them 14" x 22", then sew it all the way around except for about 4" at the top for a little opening. Then reverse it, and tuck in the top where the opening was. Stitch it all the way around two times to get a double stitching. (That makes it stay nice and flat. It's a little heavier on the edges and stays firm on the table.) These placements can go in the washing machine, in the dryer, and back on the table.

The Blue Plate

Last December my Bible study completed the year with a salad luncheon. We finished early in the month so the women could have time to prepare for the holiday and spend time with their families.

The women presented me, their teacher, with one of the best gifts I've ever received. It was a Blue Plate with beautiful white lettering surrounding the outside which says "You Are Number One Today." My heart felt warm and so very special. They were expressing their thanks and love through this unique gift. As we shared each others' salads that day, I ate off the special Blue Plate.

I discovered that the plate was hand-glazed of fine ceramic and is like no other plate. No two are exactly alike, even though a company makes them. I was now the owner of an original Blue Plate!

Knowing the feeling I received using the Blue Plate, I wanted to share that same feeling with other people. As Christmas drew near, my beautiful turkey dinner was in preparation. That Christmas day was warm and cozy, with the smell of pine and roasting turkey. Our family of 26 gathered around the buffet table for a time of praise and thanksgiving. Now was the time to present the Blue Plate to some special person in our family.

My husband Bob and I chose the most special person who came into our lives and family that year. Our daughter, Jenny, was married that September, and Craig, her new husband and our son-in-law, was the most special gift of God to us as a family. He was number one, as it was his first Christmas with us. I wish you could have seen his eyes and the cute smile that crossed his face when we announced that he was the one who got to eat Christmas dinner off the Number One Blue Plate.

More Happiness

Our Blue Plate didn't end there. As February came along, I planned a special dinner for my husband to celebrate Valentine's Day. I decided to make a "Love

Basket," filled with his favorite foods, and to have dinner in our patio, located outside our bedroom.

The card table I set up looked beautiful with a blue-and-white gingham cloth, white eyelet napkins, candle, flowers, and at Bob's place the Blue Plate saying "You Are Number One Today." I knew he was making his choice of who would be his special Valentine, and I wanted to be the one! At the sight of the table with the plate, all so simple, yet so beautiful, my Bob expressed his love and thanks for making him feel like he was my number one man. It was another way of telling him I loved him and appreciated all he did for our family.

I then discovered that our Blue Plate was an American tradition that the early American families used when someone deserved special praise or attention. God tells us in His Word that we are to encourage each other and build each other up (1 Thessalonians 5:11). Now, generations later, we can return to this custom and use it to feed on the positive. I continue to remind my Bible study women to tell *God* the negative about their husband and family, and tell the *person* the positive. Now we had another way to express that positive attitude.

When our son, Brad, turned 21, we had a family dinner to celebrate this special year. As he sat down at his place, there sat the Blue Plate, another way of telling him, "We're proud of you. We're proud that God gave us a son, and now you're a man. Bless you, our son, as you meet life with God's hand on yours."

By now we had purchased a special pen that writes on ceramic and won't wash off. So we began to list on the back of the plate the dates and special occasions it was used for. As the years pass we will always have the remembrance of all the special times and dates.

This year Bob and I discipled and counseled with two special young women. They wanted to do something special for Bob, as his birthday was drawing near, so they invited both of us out for lunch. We took the Blue Plate along, hidden in my tote bag, and asked the waitress to serve Bob his lunch off the Number One Blue Plate. What a surprise when the Blue Plate appeared in the restaurant with lunch served on it! The cook was chuckling along with all the other people that day as they watched him receive his lunch. Did he feel special? You bet!

Building the Good

By now I'm more excited than ever to build the positive and good self-esteem into others with this plate. Our plate was priceless by now and becoming a family heirloom, one we can hand down from generation to generation, especially with all the occasions and dates listed on the back.

I suggested to a mother who was in a dilemma as to what to give her son's teacher at the end of the school year the possibility of collecting 50 cents per child from the class and purchasing a Number One Blue Plate (with pen) and having all the children sign and date the back. "Great idea!" she exclaimed, and did so. As she related the opening of the gift, her eyes filled with joy as the teacher read the beautiful lettering, "You are Number One Today," and hugged the plate.

In my husband's family there are three sons: Bob, his twin brother Bill, and his younger brother Ken. Their birthdays all fall in the same month, a day apart. Bob's mother, Gertie, always makes a big celebration for their birthdays. I wanted to take the Blue Plate along, again hidden in my tote bag, but I didn't have three plates. So, thinking of a creative way to use the plate, I decided it was a natural to use it for Gertie! After our blessing I took Mom Gertie's hands and thanked her for her love and warmth over the years. What a special lady to have given us three daughters-in-law such wonderful husbands! We expressed our thanks for her time and love to all our children (her ten grandchildren). There was no doubt that she was the one that day to experience the magic of the Number One Blue Plate.

By now I'm sure you're seeing the excitement of using a plate to speak volumes of love when many times words aren't enough. Other ideas for the plate could be a job promotion, homecoming, when an old friend visits, good report card, new baby, graduation, engagement, Father's Day, anniversary, Mother's Day, winning the big game, and many others.

God bless you as you build up the positive in other people.

6
THE LOVE BASKET

A Love Basket can be used for those very special times when you want to say "I love you" in a different way. It can be filled with food for dinner at the beach or by a lake or stream, or it can be taken to a ball game, a concert, or the park. It can even be taken in your care on a love trip. It may be a surprise lunch or dinner in the backyard, in your bedroom, or under a tree, but be creative and use it to say "I love you."

What You'll Need

Here are the things you'll need in order to make a Love Basket. First of all, you'll need a basket with a handle, preferably a heavy-duty basket something like a picnic basket without a lid but having a nice sturdy handle. Then you'll need a tablecloth. It can be made from a piece of fabric or from a sheet. I generally cut them about 45" square. You'll want to line the inside of your basket with this tablecloth, letting it drape over the side so it looks real cute. I make these for wedding shower gifts, anniversary gifts, or bridal gifts.

Inside our little basket we're going to put two fancy

glasses with a stem. It's nice to use glasses with tall stems so they look pretty in the basket. We'll also need four napkins. I like to use a little print, with maybe a gingham, to make it look a little fun and different. One napkin will be for your lap and the other will be used as a napkin, but for now fluff up your napkins inside the top of the glasses so they puff up and look like a little powder puff inside your pretty little glasses.

Next you'll need to add a nice tall candleholder and a candle. I like to use something tall because it shows up from the top of your basket. You'll also need a bottle of sparkling apple cider. This is nonalcoholic, but it bubbles up very nicely. (You can buy this in the juice department of your market.) You'll also want a loaf of French bread plus some pretty fresh flowers to make the basket look really fun and inviting. Also, you'll want some cheese, salami, dill pickles, and any other good things that you really like.

Love Basket Ideas

Now let me share with you some ideas I have for my Love Basket. I've been making Love Baskets for my husband for the past 15 years. We all sense times when our husband needs a little extra attention. Maybe things have been tough at work, or maybe he's depressed over something, or maybe he just needs to feel that he's needed. Maybe you've had things out of priority, and you need to get things back into priority and to let him know that he's important in your life. These are times when you want to put together a Love Basket.

I can remember saying to my friend or neighbor, "You know, Bob needs a Love Basket tomorrow night, and I'd like to do it for him. Would you take the kids for a few hours for me while I make a Love Basket for him? The next time your husband needs a Love Basket, I'll take your kids for you." I'll tell you, they're happy to do it for you. And I'm happy to do it for anyone.

This last Valentine's Day we had a Love Basket even though the kids are grown up now. Bob and I weren't going to be able to be together on Valentine's Day, so I decided I would make a Love Basket for him the night before. That morning I called him at work and said, "Tonight I want to take you out to a special restaurant that you've never been to before that has your very favorite food." He asked, "Well, where is it?" I replied, "I'm not going to tell you. It's just a special place in town that I'm going to take you tonight. Could you be home by 6 o'clock?" Do you know what? He got home at 5:30!

What he didn't know was that during the morning I had fried up his very favorite Southern fried chicken. I had also made potato salad, fruit salad, and some yummy rolls. I had the whole dinner prepared in the morning because I didn't want the house to smell from food by the time he walked in the door that night.

Dinner on the Deck

We live in a two-story house with a deck that goes out from our bedroom that overlooks the city, with a beautiful view of everything. We had never had dinner on our deck before, so I took a card table up there, plus a couple of folding chairs. I put the red-and-white gingham tablecloth on the table, as well as the candleholder and a red candle. I put the Number One Blue Plate on his side of the table. I put a beautiful Valentine card right on the plate for him, lit a candle in our bedroom, and had the music all ready to turn on. It was the most beautiful restaurant in town. It was just gorgeous that night.

So then Bob came in. "Well, where are we going?" he asked. I replied, "It's a surprise." He asked, "Do I have to change my clothes or anything?" I said, "No, you're perfect just the way you are." So I went into the kitchen and picked up the Love Basket. (In the Love Basket were all his favorite foods, but they were covered with the cloth). I handed him the Love Basket and said, "Follow me." Bob knows now, after 15 years, that when the Love Basket comes out, really special things are going to happen. So he followed me, no doubt about that.

We went upstairs with the candle lit and the music going. As he walked out onto the deck he saw that beautiful tablecloth with the candle and the Blue Plate and the glasses and the napkins. He opened the Love Basket and took out the fried chicken plus all the other special things. So there that evening we had a beautiful meal together enjoying each other, communicating with each other, and loving each other.

Now what was I telling Bob by doing this? I was telling him that I loved him, that he was important, that I cared for him. I didn't have to tell him all I had done all day to prepare for that evening. He knew I took the time to set the table, to make it special. He knew I had worked hard to make that dinner very special to him. Do you know what he felt like? He felt like a king. He knew that he was the top priority in my life.

Jenny's Love Basket

Let me tell you a fun experience that Jenny had. She made a breakfast Love Basket for Craig when they were courting. I'll never forget the morning they were going to Los Angeles for the whole day for dental convention. Jenny put a Love Basket together with flowers, candle, candelabra, orange juice, bran muffins, fresh strawberries, and sliced canteloupe. When Craig came to pick her up at 6 A.M. he couldn't believe his eyes. He'd never seen anything like that before, especially at 6 A.M.! Later Jenny said, "Mom, it was so neat. We got in the car and I did everything. I put the napkin on his lap and we ate on the freeway and had our little Love

Basket together." Gals, this is a sure way to get a husband. At least it worked for Jenny, because five months later they were married!

Craig's Love Basket

One year later, our son-in-law Craig made a Love Basket for their first anniversary. He wanted it to be a surprise, so he put it all together with special hors d'oeuvres and hid it in the car. When Jenny came home from work he told her they needed to run a few errands. What she didn't know was that he was organized. He had planned a Love Basket over the cliffs of Corona del Mar with crashing waves below, just one hour from their home. He also had made reservations for their one-year anniversary night in a hotel in Laguna Beach.

They enjoyed their Love Basket. To Jenny's surprise, Craig had candlelight, napkins, cloth, and all. It was perfect. He then whisked her away to the hotel. When she discovered what he was doing she exclaimed, "Craig, I can't stay overnight. I have no clothes." But you see, Craig had taken care of that too. He had her clothes, beach towel, lounge chair, bathing suit, and all. However, when he got to her makeup he wasn't sure just what to bring, so you know what he did? He took out her whole makeup drawer and put it into the car. Can't you see them now, carrying the drawer into the hotel? But who cares—it was a way of showing his love to her—all because of a Love Basket.

A Letter of Love

Let me share with you a letter I received from one of the gals who attended the seminar.

Dear Emilie:

I'm still thinking about your seminar and how much food for thought you offered. Everyone had to go away with treasures in thought, word, or deed. From your testimony to your organizing and all the helpful hints, I thank you. And the Love Basket—well, that was the best of them all.

Just ask my husband. He got his first one Saturday night. He absolutely loved it, sparkling apple cider and all. Candlelight. He was so thrilled that he says he'll have to thank you personally for that one. It was so much fun that we even had ours in our bedroom. You helped me so much by just one statement you made about seeking and having the quiet and gentle spirit. God used you that night and answered my prayer for help concerning how to deal and communicate with my son. I was getting all worked up and frustrated and was arguing with him. Now I'm firm, gentle, and quiet, and it works. Thank You, Lord, and thank you, Emilie. I thought you'd like to hear that one because I want to encourage you to go on with your ministry, as it's blessing lives.

Love,
Rosemary

7

GARAGE ORGANIZATION

"Help! I'm in the garage! Over here. No, silly, not over there—in the middle of the garage, third heap on your left.

"Come fast! Help! I'm under the newspapers and magazines. Thank you! Look at all this mess. Can you believe it? We really do need to clean this garage."

What You'll Need

1. Trash bags
2. Jars—mayonnaise, peanut butter, and jelly size.
3. Small metal cabinets with plastic drawers. You can purchase these at a hardware store. This would take the place of jars.
4. Large hooks—the type you hang bicycles on.
5. Boxes—cardboard-type used for apples and oranges. Most supermarkets have them.
6. Broom and rake hooks; hardware stores will have these too.
7. One to four plastic trash cans, for uses *other* than trash.
8. Two to six empty coffee cans.

9. Black marking pen.
10. Three trash bags, marked "Put Away," "Throw Away," and "Give Away."

How to Begin

1. Set a date. Example: Saturday, 9 A.M. Call a family meeting and ask the family to help "poor mom" clean the garage.
2. Make a list of all jobs.
3. Delegate responsibilities to each member of the family. Responsibilities could be written on pieces of paper and put into a basket. Have each family member, friend, neighbor, cat, dog, or whomever you can get to help, draw three jobs from the basket.

An Example

1. Jenny: Sort the nails and screws into different jars or the metal organization cabinet with the plastic drawers you purchased last week.
2. Brad: Separate hammers, screwdrivers, wrenches, and small tools into piles, then put them into the empty coffee cans you have prelabeled with the black marking pen.
3. Husband Bob: Sort your possessions—papers, pipes, bolts, etc.—and put them into jars and cardboard boxes. Label them with the black marking pen.
4. Craig: Roll up neatly the hoses, extension cords, wires, ropes, and any other roll-up type of materials. Put all gardening tools with long handles (such as rake, shovel, edger, broom, etc) down into one of the trash cans, or hang these tools on a wall in the garage with the special hooks purchased especially for them.
5. Dori: Empty your large bag of dried dog food into another of the plastic trash cans with a tight lid. It

will keep fresh and prevent little animals such as mice from enjoying the food.

6. Mark: Your ten-year-old neighbor boy can collect all the rags, old towels, sheets, etc. and put those into a trash can with a lid or into a cardboard box marked accordingly.

7. Mom: Arrange and label the cardboard boxes, having them put on shelves (hopefully you have some) in the garage according to priority. For example: you don't need the Christmas ornament boxes on the lower shelf because you will only get them down once a year, so they should be put on a top shelf.

More Suggestions

Bicycles can be hung on rafters with the large hooks you purchased at the hardware store. Most regular cars will easily drive under them. These are for bicycles not used every day. Maybe Dad or an older son could make a bike rack for the other bikes used often.

The partially used bags of cement, fertilizer, and other dry materials can also be stored in the plastic trash cans with lids. This will prevent the materials from getting wet.

Gardening pots, bricks, flats, etc. can be neatly stored on a shelf in the garage or outside garage in a convenient spot. Or build a few shelves outside just for those things. Winter weather won't hurt them, and you have little need for them during those months anyway.

We must not forget the trash bags marked "Put Away," "Throw Away," and "Give Away." Be sure to fill them. You'll be finding newspapers, magazines, and empty or dried-up cans of paint. Put those types of things in the Throw Away trash bag. And throw them away!

You will also find many items which are perfectly good but which you never or seldom use. Put these into the Give Away bag and divide them up among neighbors, youth groups, needly families, thrift shops, churches, etc., or else have a garage sale and make a little extra money.

Whenever we have a garage sale we let the children keep what money comes from their items, such as outgrown games and toys, ice skates, clothing, etc. This encourages them to clean out and get rid of little used items. Be careful, however, because children can get over excited and sell their bed, desk, cat, or even baby brother!

The Put Away trash bag will have items you'll need to store in cardboard boxes, such as athletic equipment (mitts, baseballs, baseball caps, Frisbees, cleats, etc.). Another box will house the winter ice skates, mittens, snow caps, ski sweaters, thermal underwear, and socks. Be sure to throw in a few mothballs and to label the boxes as to what's inside.

Another good way to label the boxes is to mark the items on a 3" x 5" white card and tape or staple them on the front of the boxes.

When storing clothing, you may want to put them in a small trash bag with a few whole cloves, then into the cardboard storage box. This prevents silverfish and other little critters from having a picnic.

Spray paint cans and smaller paint cans can be put into a storage box and labeled too.

Are you beginning to feel all boxed up? Great! That will free you from the guilt feelings of garage disorganization, and you'll now know where everything is.

Sweep and hose out any leftovers. Put hamburgers on the barbecue, then kick back and enjoy your family, being thankful that you worked well together!

8
KITCHEN ORGANIZATION

Do you realize that one of the reasons you're crying for kitchen organization is because you spend on an average of 1092 hours a year in the kitchen? That's a lot of hours in an area that definitely needs to be organized.

What You'll Need

First you'll need some jars. You can start by collecting mayonnaise jars. Those little marinated-artichoke jars are also great to store things in. Tupperware is a wonderful thing to have as well. If you don't have it, maybe you need to get invited to a Tupperware party and start getting some Tupperware pieces that you can use. Those lazy Susan turntables are also super.

Also get some contact paper, some newspapers, or anything that you can cover some boxes with. You'll also need some trash bags, plus a felt marker pen and some labels.

Scheduling Time

The next crucial thing is to schedule a time. Here's what I recommend: Set the timer on your stove for 15 minutes, then work like mad until the timer goes off. Then do whatever else you have to. If you're working toward a deadline, you have a tendency to move a little faster. So schedule yourself a time in the day when you're going to organize your kitchen.

Proverbs 16:3 says that we are to commit our works to the Lord, and then they will succeed. If we are in a position to make a commitment to organizing our kitchen, we need to pray about it. God is interested in the very tiny things about us, even getting the cupboards cleaned in the kitchen. So commit your works to Him. Ask Him to give you the time and enthusiasm you need to put this into practice.

In the Kitchen

So now we're in the kitchen. First let's get some of our cupboard doors open. We don't want to open every single one of them because we'll be knocking our heads and passing out, but we need to start with, let's say, the upper cupboards. So we open all those up and start pulling everything out, starting with the cupboards closest to the sink (because these are the ones we get in and out of the most and are probably in the biggest mess.) We'll want to take everything out, get all the shelves wiped out, and then repaper them, perhaps using contact paper. Maybe we'll also want to repaint the shelves.

Then eliminate those things you want to throw out. You know you have things in your kitchen that you've been storing for a long time but haven't been using, such as broken dishes, mugs, and vases, plus cleansers and other things that are partially used but you'll never use again. You may want to give those away or throw them away, but in either case get rid of them.

Next you have items that you use daily. For these buy a turntable that is made specifically for using underneath your kitchen sink. You can put all your cleansers and so forth on this handy item.

Now for the things you're not using. Put these in either your Throw Away bag or your Give Away bag, or else in a box that you use as a kitchen overflow. (Mark some of your boxes "Kitchen Overflow." You may need several of these.) These seldom used boxes can be stored in the garage shelves where you have extra room.

Equipment Priorities

Priority use means that those things which you use all the time will go back into the cupboard. Such things as spices, dishes, pots and pans, etc., should be put back nicely and neatly. I use lazy Susan turntables for my spices. I don't think you can have enough of them. Or you can use a spice rack. (A spice rack also comes in handy for vitamin bottles.)

The things you don't use very often should go back in the cupboards, on the highest shelves. This might include such things as your big platters for your Thanksgiving turkey. (You might use this only once or twice a year.)

Then get your broken appliances repaired. They're sitting around waiting for somebody to pay attention to them. Those that cost more than half the cost of a new appliance should be thrown out.

For you that have high school students going into college, save your appliances that are a little old-fashioned or just extra. Put them in a box and store them away. We found that when our children went off to college they started getting their own apartments, and they wanted such things as the extra iron, toaster, etc. So start saving these things for them. Put them in a box, label them, and number them. Then put this information in your card files.

Kitchen Overflow

Now for your overflow. At one time Bob and I and the

children lived in a condominium. We had moved from a big two-story house to a small three-bedroom condominium. I found that when I was organizing the kitchen I didn't have a place for everything. That's when I discovered what I call the kitchen overflow. If you're lucky enough to have a shelf or cabinets in the garage, that's a good place to put the overflow. If not, get some of those nice boxes with lids and put the overflow in them. The overflow might include such things as a waffle iron, an extra set of dishes, or even extra canned goods.

Many of you may be living in apartments, mobile homes or other smaller quarters where you don't have a lot of cupboard space. This has been one of the complaints that I've heard from women. "What do I do with all this stuff? I don't have enough room for it." Well, when they're in nice uniform boxes they can go in a bedroom or closet or out in the garage somewhere.

What should you do with gadgets and utensils if you're short of space? Put them in a crock and tie a cute little bow around it. It looks cute on the counter, and all your whips and wooden spoons and spatulas can probably fit in it. Set the crock close to the stove or at some other handy spot.

Unavoidable Junk

Then there are the junk drawers. There is no way to eliminate these, so don't feel you have to get rid of that junk drawer, because we all have them. The problem is, they are usually very junky. So we can take that junk and pretty well clean it up. My junk drawer has one of these little silverware sectional containers. They come in all colors. In it I put the hammer, the screwdriver, and a couple of those little artichoke jars in which I keep some cup hooks, some nails, some screws, some thumbtacks—all those little things. You may want to get two

or three of these jars to put in your junk drawer so you'll
have everything fairly organized when you pull it out.
(The reason why jars are nice is because you can see
what's inside of them.)

Another nice thing is an egg carton. These are fabulous to use for those little screws. You can cut apart the
cartons so that you have small sections of egg cartons.
Then the little screws, hooks, etc., can fit in there and go
nicely in your junk drawer. Another neat thing to do
with an egg carton is to open it up and put it in the bottom of the paper bag you use as a garbage can liner. It
absorbs the moisture and takes care of all the gunky stuff
that falls to the bottom. Then when the children take
out the bag, it won't fall apart and drip all over the kitchen.

I've found that it's not really what you do that makes
you tired, but what you don't do. The mental pressure
that we have about all those things we need to do makes
us worry and become concerned, and we get tired over
it. So we need to get moving and do the job.

Pantry Space

You're lucky if you have a pantry. If you don't have a
pantry, you may have a cupboard in your kitchen that
you're using as a pantry. Not many of us are fortunate
enough to have a walk-in pantry like Grandma used to
have, where she could put all her bowls and flour and
sugar. I've opened women's pantries, not to see what's
there but just to get something out for someone, and I've
found all kinds of toys, books, etc. that should be in
other parts of the house. If you have small children and
need to keep some of their things in the pantry, then get
something like a plastic laundry basket to keep all their
toys in.

Potatoes or onions can be kept in colored plastic stack
trays. These are also wonderful to use in closets in your

bedrooms, particularly for your children. You can stack and fold their T-shirts and underwear in one of these, and you can keep all their little socks (rolled up) in another one. You can actually have four or five of these going at the same time.

Making the Pantry Cute

The pantry can be organized in a really fun and cute way. You can label the shelves with one of those tape labelers. (Maybe you already have one.) I have a friend who has everything labeled in her pantry—where the soups go, where the ketchup goes, etc. Why does she do that? Because she has older children who put her groceries away when they come in from the market. Also, she entertains a lot, and various people put things back in the pantry. I have another friend whose husband has taken little dowels, and fastened them along the shelf of the pantry so that the canned goods slide in. That's real organization!

For packaged items, such as dried taco mix, salad dressings, gravies, etc., get a shoebox and cover it with the wallpaper from your kitchen or extra wallpaper that you have or contact paper, and it will look cute in the pantry. You can also purchase plastic or metal sliding shelves. They're not as inexpensive as the other things I've mentioned, but they make for a neat pantry.

Jar everything you can. My jars in the pantry have everything in them. (You might go to a fast-food place and ask for some of those big mustard and mayonnaise jars.) Put everything you can in jars—rice, Bisquick, popcorn, beans, sugar, flour, graham crackers, cookies, raisins, coffee filters, dog biscuits—everything.

We had a problem because the mice liked the dog biscuits out in the garage, and I was finding those cute little leavings around. So I took a big jar and put the dog biscuits in it. This way we got rid of the mice, and the biscuits look real cute in the jar!

Work Together, Store Together

Things that work together should be stored together. What does that mean? If you're going to organize baking items—your mixing bowls, your hand mixer, your measuring cups—all those things can be stored in one little area together. I bake homemade bread, so I have on my shelf all those things that I use to bake the bread. I have my pans, the oil, the honey, the flour, the yeast, etc. handy, so that when I'm ready to bake bread I don't have to be running from cupboard to cupboard trying to find things. After I bake the bread I put everything back together. Once the things in your kitchen have a place, then they should go back to that place. Once they find their little place, and your family gets used to it, they will begin to put things back in their areas.

Knives and Pans

Get your knives sharpened up, because you have a problem when you pick up a knife that's dull. If you never use a particular knife, throw it out.

Pots and pans should be kept neatly somewhere near the stove. You can line the shelves for the pots with plain or light-colored paper, maybe brown paper. I bought some rubber pads to keep my frying pans and other heavy potware from scratching and ruining my shelf lining. Determine the best possible position for your pans, because those are things you use often and need to get out quickly. You can draw a circle or square the size of the pan with a black felt pen, then write the pan size inside the circle or square. For example, here is where the 9-inch frying pan goes and that's where the 2-quart saucepan goes. If you have people doing things in your kitchen other than yourself, this is a wonderful way for them to know where things are to be stored.

The Refrigerator

What about the refrigerator? If you're working

through your card file, you'll remember that a refrigerator only needs to be cleaned once a month. So the first week of every month you're going to clean your refrigerator. (You have one whole week to clean it.) Look at that refrigerator as just another closet, because basically that's what it is—a cold-storage closet.

Your vegetables can be put in your Tupperware or plastic containers or baggies. The cheese and meats go on the coldest shelf. Put them in see-through containers also. You can even put some of these things in jars if you like. And remember to rotate your eggs.

Lazy Susans are great space-savers in your refrigerator. I have two of them. One is on the top shelf and stores the milk and the half-and-half. The other one has the sour cream, the cottage cheese, etc.

You can also buy dispensers and bottle racks for your refrigerator. Can dispensers are good if you use a lot of soft drinks. Some dispensers you can set right onto the shelf in your refrigerator, and they just dispense right there. There are also special milk dispensers, juice dispensers, and so forth. Your children will absolutely love these, so if you buy a dispenser for the first time, put something really healthful in it, such as milk or orange juice, because they'll love to drink out of it. They'll want to drink just to use the dispenser.

The Freezer

Now what about the freezer? When I go to the market and come home with hamburger meat, I prepare that meat to put into the freezer. I make up patties and I stick them on a cookie sheet and put them right into the freezer. They'll freeze in an hour or two. Then, as soon as they're frozen, I take them out and put them in either a baggie or a plastic container, so that when I'm ready a week later to get the hamburger out of the freezer, they don't stick together. This way I can bring out two hamburger patties or ten patties. If I'm going to make meatloaf, I just take out five or six hamburger patties and make them into meatloaf.

Keep ahead of your ice cubes, especially if it's summertime and you don't have an icemaker. Bag up some ice cubes and put them in the freezer so you'll have extras when you need them.

All your frozen vegetables should be put in one section and your meats in another section. All your casseroles that you premake can also be put together. When I make a lasagna casserole or spaghetti sauce, I make enough for tonight plus one for the freezer. And I always label and date these things so I'll know how long they've been in the freezer.

I also try to keep emergency meals in the freezer in case company drops in or I've been too busy to prepare anything else. You can buy little plastic containers especially for making TV dinners. With these, if you have leftovers from the meal, you can put together one little TV dinner with foil around the top, then label it and put it into the freezer. When you get four or five of these accumulated, you've got a nice meal for everyone and maybe something a little different.

Be sure you label things that go into the freezer, because otherwise you'll find mystery packages in the freezer as you clean it out. It's amazing how things change when they're frozen! They don't look the same!

Ice cream and frozen desserts should go together in your freezer. Did you know that you can freeze potato chips, corn chips, tortillas, muffins, and bread? If you use wheat flour, be sure to keep that in the freezer so it will keep nice and fresh. Candles should also be kept in the freezer, particularly if you've bought them at a discount price. (If you keep them in the freezer, the won't drip or pop on you.)

This and That

Let's talk about some miscellaneous items. Kitchen towels and cloths should be kept in a drawer or on a shelf that's close at hand, and pot holders near the point of use. Anytime you can put anything on a rack, it will be a space-saver for you. The plastic racks come in all sizes and are very inexpensive. For example, your dishes can go on plate-holders especially designed for that purpose.

I keep a Lazy Susan under every bathroom sink in the house. The shampoos, the hair sprays, and all of those things can go on a Lazy Susan. The cleaning products can go in a little basket or bucket. This way everything is right there in one container that you can pick up and take with you when you're cleaning throughout the house.

Keep a coffee can full of baking soda near the stove in case of a grease fire, and label the can with a felt-tip pen. Be sure to teach your children what the baking soda is for and how to use it.

Always load your sharp knives in the dishwasher with the blades down. Teach your children to do this also, so they don't cut themselves. All of us have cut ourselves at one time or another on a freshly sharpened knife, so we need to be careful with cutlery. Don't cook over an open flame in billowing long sleeves. Don't, for example, go into the kitchen in your negligee and start cooking over the open flame. Be sure to roll up your sleeves.

Joyful in the Process

First Thessalonians 5:16-18 says, "Always be joyful. Always keep on praying. No matter what happens, always be thankful for this is God's will for you who belong to Christ Jesus"(TLB). We sometimes become overwhelmed with our homes as we struggle from "total mess to total rest." Some of you haven't gotten it done. But that's okay as long as you're in the process. This is particularly true of your kitchen. It can become overwhelming for you. You've got a lot of things to organize, and maybe not a lot of room to put them. So don't let it become overwhelming.

God says that we are to be joyful in our homes and around our husbands. So we need to keep on praying no matter what happens. Sometimes we don't feel like having an attitude of prayer in our homes, and that's when we need to ask God to give us that joyful attitude no matter what happens. We need to continue with an attitude of prayer as we organize our kitchen.

Another wonderful thing to do is to turn on some good music. If you have any good Christian tapes or good Christian radio stations, turn them on and allow God to speak to you through His music as you move in the organization of your home.

You spend a lot of time in your home, so make it a joyful place. Pray about your attitude toward your kitchen and your meals and the presentation of those meals to your family. Then let the music flow in your heart because of the love of our Lord Jesus Christ.

Kitchen Organization Outline
This is the day which the Lord has made; let us rejoice and be glad in it.
(Psalm 118:24 NASB)

EQUIPMENT NEEDED
- Jars (assorted sizes, peanut butter, mayonnaise, artichoke)
- Tupperware
- Rubbermaid Lazy Susans & turntables
- Large cardboard box—labeled KITCHEN OVERFLOW
- Contact paper

- Trash bag marked THROW AWAY
- Felt marker pen
- Labels

SCHEDULE A FREE TIME
Commit your work to the Lord;
then it will succeed.
(Proverbs 16:3 TLB)

A. Open all cupboard doors.
   1. Begin with cupboard closest to sink.
   2. Take EVERYTHING out.
   3. Wipe out shelves and re-paper with contact paper if needed.
   4. Eliminate, throw away or put aside any item that is not being used daily or bi-daily. (Example: odd mugs, glasses, plastic forks, utensils).
B. Prime-time equipment goes back into cupboards
   —Spices used often
   —Glasses
   —Dishes
   —Pots and pans, etc.
C. Seldom-used equipment goes to the back of the cupboard or the highest shelves.
D. Put aside broken appliances to be repaired, or get rid of them now.

OVERFLOW
Box or shelve in garage: odd vases, dishes, platters, pans, camping equipment (can be put into own marked box), canned goods, seldom-used appliances (waffle iron, coffee pot, juicer, blender).

GADGETS UTENSILS

Put wooden spoons, ladles, long-handled spoons, forks, potato masher into a crock or ceramic pot. Saves space.

JUNK DRAWERS

Get plastic divider (usually used for flatware). Use for such things as a small hammer, thumbtacks, small plastic box or small jar with nails, cup hooks, screwdriver, pliers, tweezers, glue, flashlight batteries, fuses, matches, scissors, and other miscellaneous items. Plastic egg cartons, when cut, make great organizers.

*It's not what you do that makes you
tired, but what you don't do.*

PANTRY

Lucky is you have one—*it's for food only.* Not papers, books, or toys!

A. Sort out food items.
B. Label shelf to indicate food items:
   Soups, fruits, vegetables, cereals, salad dressings. Baking section includes flour, sugar, baking soda, mixes.
C. Packaged items, such as dry taco mix, salad dressing, gravy, etc. should be put into a large jar or small shoebox covered with contact paper or wallpaper.
D. Jar everything you can—tea bags, plastic spoons & forks, nuts, flour, cereal, sugar, chips, croutons, beans, noodles, rice, oatmeal, popcorn, spaghetti, graham crackers, cookies, raisins, coffee filters, dog biscuits.

THINGS THAT WORK TOGETHER SHOULD BE STORED TOGETHER.

A. Baking items, mixing bowls, hand mixer, measuring cups, etc.
B. Coffeepot, filters, coffee and perhaps mugs.

SHARPEN DULL KNIVES OR THROW THEM OUT

POTS & PANS

A. To keep neatly, line shelves with plain or light-colored paper.
B. Determine best possible position.
C. Draw an exaggerated outline of the item on the shelf paper with a magic marker. You can also write the pan's description within its borders.

REFRIGERATOR

A. Look at it as just another closet.
B. Fruits, vegetables should be put into plastic containers with lids or plastic baggies, or in refrigerator drawers.
C. Cheese and meats go on coldest shelf (use all types of see-through containers with tight lids).
D. Eggs—remember to rotate oldest to front or to the right depending on whether you have a drawer or shelf for eggs.
E. Lazy Susans, a space-saver, will hold sour cream, cottage cheese, jellies, peanut butter, yogurt, mustard. A Lazy Susan on the top shelf will hold milk, half-and-half, orange juice jar, or bottle of cold water.
F. You can also buy can dispensers and bottle racks which attach to refrigerator shelf.

FREEZER

A. Hamburger meat shaped into patties. Freeze on cookie sheet and then transfer to plastic bags. They won't stick together that way. (They thaw quickly for meal loaf, burger patties, tacos, casseroles, or spaghetti sauce.)
B. Keep ahead of ice cubes. Periodically baggie up a bunch and store them.
C. Frozen packaged vegetables all go together.
D. Date and label all leftovers. AVOID MYSTERY PACKAGES. They store great in Zip Lock bags, or wrap tight with foil to avoid freezer burn.
E. Ice cream and frozen desserts go together.
F. Potato chips, corn chips, nuts, breads, muffins, wheat flour, tortillas, flour, corn and candles (keep them from dripping) all freeze well.
G. Make ahead: lasagna, noodle and cheese casseroles, soups, beans, spaghetti sauce, enchiladas. BE SURE TO DATE AND LABEL. Also, if you are freezing in jars, be sure to leave 1½" at the top to allow for expansion.

MISCELLANEOUS

A. Kitchen towels and cloths.
  1. Put in drawer or shelf close to sink.
  2. Pot holders near point of use.
B. Racks.
  1. They double dish space and cupboard space.
  2. Plastic utensil drawers can be purchased at hardware-type store at low expense.
  3. They come in various sizes and will fit together.
  4. Can also be used in bathroom and bedroom drawers.
C. Cleaning products should be put in one area with dustcloths and a few rags. Include window cleaner,

waxes, Comet-type cleaners.
D. Keep a coffee can full of baking soda near stove in case of a grease fire. BE SURE TO LABEL.
E. Always load sharp knives into dishwasher, blade down.
F. Don't cook over open flames with billowing long sleeves or flowing night robe.

> *Always be joyful. Always keep on*
> *praying. No matter what happens,*
> *always be thankful, for this is God's*
> *will for you who belong to Christ Jesus.*
> (1 Thessalonians 5:16-18 TLB)

9

WARDROBE ORGANIZATION

Now let's get into our closet and get organized. Let's weed out some of those things we don't need and get our closets in order.

The Right Equipment

As we get into our wardrobe we'll need some equipment with which to get organized. First we'll need some boxes with lids. Then we'll need some materials to cover shoeboxes. (Shoes that you don't wear often can go in shoeboxes covered with leftover wallpaper and labeled with a felt-tip pen. This way you'll have a nice-looking closet instead of just having funny-looking shoe boxes lying around.)

Then you may want to get some clear plastic boxes. In these you can put your scarves and belts and little clutch bags. Then get some plastic hangers. Get rid of those wire hangers that are always getting tangled together and get instead some cute little plastic hangers in different colors. (You may want to color coordinate your wardrobe.) A great way to save space is to get a slack rack. You can hang up to five pairs of pants on one of these, and it will take up the space of just one pair of pants in your closet. These are also wonderful to hang your tablecloths on. (As you make your tablecloths out of your sheets, just hang them on a slack rack.)

You'll also need some storage boxes for these clothes that you really want to keep but are not using right now.

Getting Started

How do we get started? Let's get those trash bags again. We'll go through the same concept that we did with the "Total Mess to Total Rest" program. We get three trash bags and label them "Put Away," "Give Away," and "Throw Away." As we walk into each closet we take everything out and get vicious again.

As you pull those things out of your closet, keep in mind that if you haven't worn it for the past year it goes in one of those three bags. Either you're going to put it away somewhere else, or you're going to give it away to somebody else, or you're going to throw it away. If you haven't worn it for two or three years, you'll definitely have to give it away or throw it away.

Taking Inventory

Now let's start taking inventory. (You can use the Wardrobe Inventory sheet printed in this chapter.) As you begin to take your inventory, you'll quickly begin to see what you have. For example, you may have way too many navy-blue pants. You only need one pair of good navy-blue pants and maybe a couple pairs of nice jeans. So you can begin to see where you've made your mistakes as your take your wardrobe inventory, and you'll be able to start correcting those mistakes.

Everything in its Place

Hang your things up as you put them back into your closet. Each thing should have a definite place. For example, all the extra hangers can go at the left end of your closet. Then arrange all your blouses according to color, then your pants, then your skirts, etc. If you have a jacket that matches your pants, separate them. (Hang the jacket with the jackets and the pants with the pants.) This way you can mix or match your things and not always wear the same jacket and pants together.

Your shoes can go on shoe racks. Some neat different kinds of shoe racks are now available, or you can cover shoeboxes with wallpaper or Christmas paper. (Your children can help you do this.)

Your smaller handbags can go in clear plastic boxes. The larger ones can go up on the shelf above your wardrobe. A hanging plastic shoebag is great, because you can also put your purses and scarves in it. Belts and ties should go on hooks. Ribbons can be hung on these hooks too. Or you can just hammer a big nail into the closet wall. You'd be surprised at how many belts you can get on a nail!

Boxes Again

Be sure to number your boxes. If you're using file cards, number each card to correspond with the number of the box holding your extra clothing. Then list on the card what you have in the box.

Do It!

Be sure you give away things you're not using. Many people today are tight with their finances and can't afford some things. If you have things that you aren't wearing, give them to someone who will be able to use them. They'll be grateful to you, and you'll feel good about your giving.

Wardrobe Organization Outline

EQUIPMENT NEEDED
- 3 to 10 large boxes with lids or 3 large trash bags
- Materials to cover shoe boxes, such as wallpaper, contact paper, or even fabric.
- Clear plastic boxes for scarves, and clutch handbags.
- Plastic hangers, all one color if you like
- 2 to 4 hooks
- Belt or tie holder
- 2 to 6 storage boxes

HOW TO GET STARTED
A. Label boxes (trash bags)
   1. Put away
   2. Throw away
   3. Give away
B. Plan a one- to two-hour time, and think toward an orderly closet.
   1. Take everything out on floor and shelves.
   2. Get vicious and make decisions.
   3. Put items in proper boxes. The rule to guide you is: If you haven't worn it for one year, it must be put away somewhere else or given away. If for two years, it doesn't belong in the closet, and if for three years or longer give away or throw away. (There might be a very few exceptions.)
   4. Use your Wardrobe Inventory Sheet.
      a. Return items to your closet and list them on your Wardrobe Inventory Sheet.
      b. Suggested order for your clothes:
         1. Extra hangers
         2. Blouses
         3. Pants
         4. Skirts

WARDROBE INVENTORY

Blouses	Pants	Skirts	Jackets	Sweaters

Dresses	Gowns	Lingerie	Shoes	Jewelry

Things I Never Wear

Needs

    5. Blazers & Jackets
    6. Sweaters (these can also be folded and
       put on shelf or in a drawer)
    7. Dresses
    8. Gowns
 c. For each item, all colors together (example: light
   to dark)
 d. Coats and heavy jackets can be kept in a hall
   closet or extra wardrobe closet.
 e. Shoes:
    1. Shoe racks—floor type or hanging
    2. Covered shoeboxes can be put on shelf or
       neatly stacked on floor.
 f. Handbags:
    1. Smaller ones in clear plastic boxes
    2. Larger ones on shelf above wardrobe
    3. A hanging plastic shoebag is also
       great for your handbags. Can be pur-
       chased in notions at any department
       store.
 g. Belts and ties:
    1. Belt rack applied to wall with screws
    2. Hooks are great and easy to use and
       attach.

NOTES ABOUT HANGERS

A. Wire hangers are messy and they crease clothing.
   Toss and replace them as you can with plastic or
   cloth-covered hangers.
B. Hang skirt on proper skirt hangers with clothespin-
   type clips.
C. Pants can be hung on a shirt hanger or folded in half
   over a plastic pant hanger.

STORAGE—PUT AWAY BOXES OR TRASH BAGS
A. Get boxes with lids and number each box.

B. Assign each box a 3x5 card with corresponding number. For example:

Box
#1— Jenny's summer shorts, T-shirts, skirts, sandals

Box
#2— Costume clothing: 50's outfit, black-and-white saddles, purple angora sweater w/ holes, high school cheerleader's outfit

Box
#3— Ski clothes, socks, underwear, pants, sweaters

Box
#4— Scarves, belts, jewelry, honeymoon penoir, etc. etc.

GIVE AWAY

A. Better clothing can be given to friends or family.
B. Thrift shops, Goodwill-type stores, rummage sales, church, missionaries.
C. You may want to have a co-op garage sale or clothes sale.

THROW AWAY

Put items in trash bag with twistie and set out for the trash.

10
JOBS CHILDREN CAN DO

Delegating responsibility to children is such an important aspect of motherhood that you should be giving your children responsibilities at a very young age. Make it fun for them; make games out of it. A three-year-old can dress himself, put his pajamas away, brush his hair, brush his teeth, and make his bed. You can begin to teach your children these things when they're as young as two and three years old. Some more examples: folding clothes, emptying the dishwasher (they may need some help with that—begin by having them unload some of the plastic things), clearing some of the dishes off the table (begin by teaching them to carry things back into the kitchen), emptying wastebaskets, or picking up toys before bedtime (plastic baskets are excellent for toys).

Our Responsibility
Proverbs 22:6 says, "Train up a child in the way he should go, and when he is old he will not depart from it." It is our responsibility as Christian parents to train our children and direct them and guide them in the

ways that they should go, so that when they become adults they're not domestic invalids. It's important that we give our children responsibilities and train them up. A five-year-old can set the table, clean the bathrooms, and help clean and straighten drawers and closets. As you go through your home, take your little one with you and begin to show him what you're doing. Often children don't even realize that there's toothpaste on the mirror in the bathroom, because they've never been told that they have to wipe it up. They think it just somehow automatically disappears.

Here are some more things children can do: Clean up after the pet, feed the cat, walk the dog, dust the furniture. They may do a sloppy job of dusting, and you may just say you'll have to go back and do it over, but don't go back and do it until tomorrow. Let them move the dust around a little so they at least can see the responsibilities that their moms are fulfilling. Many of you work outside your home, then have to do a full-time job at home. So you need to delegate these responsibilities to your children.

Seven and Up

Seven-year-olds can empty garbage, sweep walks, help in the kitchen after dinner, and prepare lunches for school. (If a child makes his own lunch he's not too likely to complain about it!) Then have them help clean out the car. Don't forget that they're making messes in the car as you're driving them around. You'll find that when their friends get in the car and your children are the ones that have to clean up the car they'll say to their friends, "We don't drop things in our car."

A seven-year-old can begin to learn to iron. When our daughter Jenny was eight years old she was doing all the laundry in our home, from washing it to putting it in the dryer (or hanging it up) to folding it. These are things that children can learn to do. It even helps their physical coordination to learn how to do these things.

An eight-year-old can learn to wash the bathroom mirrors, wash the windows, wash the floors in small areas, and polish shoes. As the children grow older they can be given more and more responsibilities, such as washing the car, mowing the lawn, making the dessert, painting, and cleaning the refrigerator. (Give them some ideas about refrigerators, and let them be creative.)

When our children were growing up we would delegate to each of them one night a week when they would completely prepare that meal. It could be their choice or it could be on the Menu Planner, but they were to completely make the meal. If you do this, you'll find that your children can be creative when you didn't even know they had it in them.

Teaching Our Children

Deuteronomy 6:5-7 says, "You shall love the Lord your God with all your heart and with all your soul and with all your might. And these words which I am commanding you today shall be upon your heart; and you shall teach them diligently to your sons and shall talk of them when you sit in your house and when you walk by the way and when you lie down and when you rise up." It is our responsibility as parents to be teaching our children in all areas—to teach them as we're in the kitchen, to teach them about God's creation when we're bicycling together, to teach them to make a lunch and to picnic, or go to the park or to the beach. We're to teach them many things as we build our home around our family, and as we organize and become creative.

We by ourselves cannot do it all in our homes (when we try we become frustrated), so when we begin to delegate responsibilities to our children and allow them to do some of the work for us, they begin to feel as if they are a vital part of the family. I have found that families that work together and play together will also love together, pray together, and worship God together. Then we'll raise children who are balanced people, who will become creative adults with wonderful homes of their own.

Jobs For Your Children
Children are a gift from God;
they are His reward.
(Psalm 127:3 TLB)

THREE-YEAR-OLD

1. Get dressed, put pajamas away.
2. Brush hair
3. Brush teeth
4. Make bed
5. Fold clothes and small items
6. Empty dishwasher (need help)
7. Clear meal dishes
8. Empty wastebaskets
9. Pick up toys before bed

> *Train up a child in the way*
> *he should go, and when he is*
> *old he will not depart from it.*
> (Proverbs 22:6)

FIVE-YEAR-OLD

1. Set table
2. Clean bathroom

3. Help clean and straighten drawers and closets
4. Clean up after pet
5. Feed pet
6. Walk dog
7. Dust furniture in room
8. Vacuum room
9. Help put groceries away

SEVEN-YEAR-OLD

1. Empty garbage
2. Sweep walks
3. Help in kitchen after dinner
4. Help make lunch for school
5. Schoolwork
6. Clean out car
7. Piano lessons, etc.
8. Iron flat items

EIGHT-YEAR-OLD

1. Wash bathroom mirrors
2. Wash windows
3. Wash floors in small area
4. Polish shoes

As your children grow, more responsibility can be given to them:

1. Wash car
2. Mow lawn
3. Make dessert
4. Paint
5. Clean refrigerator
6. Yardwork
7. Ironing
8. Fix an entire meal
9. Do grocery shopping

You shall love the Lord your God
with all you heart and with all your soul
and with all your might. And these words which I
am commanding you today shall be on your heart;
and you shall teach them diligently to your sons
and shall talk of them when you sit in your
house and when you walk by the way and when you
lie down and when you rise up.
(Deuteronomy 6:5-7 NASB)

11
PRAYER ORGANIZATION

Some of you may not have a prayer life at all. Others of you may have a very vital prayer life. Some of you want to have a prayer life but are fumbling with it because you don't know how to incorporate it into your life or how to organize it. I was once in that position. I was fumbling in my prayer life because I didn't know the steps to take. So that's what we want to discuss now—some steps to take in order to set up a prayer notebook and to organize our prayer life.

A Precious Letter
Let me share with you a letter that I received.

Dear Friend:

I just had to send you a note to tell you how much I love you and care about you. I saw you yesterday as you were walking with your friend. I waited all day, hoping you would want to talk with me also. As the evening drew near I gave you a sunset to close your day and a cool breeze to rest you. I waited, but you never came. It hurt me, but I still love you because I'm your friend. I saw you fall asleep, and I longed to touch your brow, so I spilled some moonlight on your pillow and on your face. Again I waited, wanting to rush down so that we could talk. I have so many gifts for you, but you awakened late the next day and rushed off to work, and my tears were in vain.

Today you look so sad and so all alone, and it makes my heart ache because I understand. My friends let me down and hurt me so many times too, but I love you. Oh, if you would only listen to me! I really love you. I try to tell you this in the blue sky and in the quiet green grass. I whisper it in the trees and breathe it in the colors of the flowers. I shout it to you in the mountain streams and give the birds love songs to sing. I clothe you with warm sunshine and give you perfume in the air with nature's scent. My love for you is deeper than the ocean and bigger than the biggest want or need in your heart. If you only knew how much I want to help you.

I want you to meet my Father. He wants to help you too. My Father is that way, you know. Just call me, ask me, talk with me—I have so much to share with you yet. I won't hassle you; I'll wait, because I love you.

> Your Friend,
> Jesus

You see, we don't take the necessary time to give to our Lord in prayer and communication. But do you know what? He loves us anyway. He loves us unconditionally. And so that's why we need to pull together some type of system in our lives where we can spend valuable time in prayer. It doesn't have to be long, either. Sometimes we get turned off because we feel it takes so much time, but it doesn't have to be long.

How to Get Started

As with everything else, we need the proper tools and materials. I would recommend a small notebook, perhaps a 5½" x 8½" three-ring binder. Get some colored little tabs, some paper, some dividers, and a pen.

Be sure to have your Bible handy. Sometimes you may want a little Bible study with yourself as you go into your prayer time, so it's always nice to have your Bible with you. As I pray, I find that many times God reveals something to me in His Word. If I'm praying for someone, I sometimes feel really convicted. Maybe I should drop that person a note and tell him I'm praying for him, supporting him in whatever. At times like this I like to be able to give a Bible verse. So it's nice to have your Bible close by.

Colossians 4:2 says that we are to devote ourselves to prayer, keeping alert in it with an attitude of thanksgiving (NASB). Our attitude as we come to the Lord should be one of thanksgiving. Christ is waiting for us. His attitude is love to us. And so our attitude in return should be one of thanksgiving.

Why Should We Pray?

Why do we pray? We pray because we want to communicate with God. In Luke 18:1 Jesus said that people ought to pray always, without giving up. Prayer also gives us an opportunity to confess to God those things that we feel guilty about. First John 1:9 says, "If we confess our sins to Him, He can be depended on to forgive us and to cleanse us from every wrong" (TLB). We can open our heart to God and confess the very worst things in our lives down to the very smallest things. God hears us, and nobody else has to know those things. This begins to teach us discipline, because when we pray we're disciplined in knowing that we are in the hand of God and that God is there to touch us, to feed us, and to give us those things which He wants us to have. This draws us closer to the Lord. As we begin to pray even briefly we begin to draw on that fellowship that we have with Christ.

Prayer keeps us from being selfish. It keeps us from looking at ourselves, and the things *we* want. When we begin to pray for someone else we remove ourselves from "me" and we gear into the other person, to love the other person. Prayer also keeps us from temptation and disobedience to God. As we pray we draw closer to God, and as we draw closer to God we find that we want to do what God wants for us. We want to be the woman that God wants us to be.

How Should We Pray

Luke 22:41 says that Jesus knelt and began to pray. This doesn't mean that every time you pray you have to get on your knees, though there are times when you will want to do this. But be flexible. We have a tendency to think that we have to keep asking God for something over and over, but Matthew 6:7 says, "Don't recite the same prayer over and over." We can give our needs to God without constantly reminding Him of them, since He already knows all about them. So if we don't pray for that thing every day, God still knows. We may pray for it once a week or once a month.

A woman I met in Newport Beach had prayed for her husband for 35 years. I'm sure she didn't get down on her knees every day and pray fervently for her husband for 15 minutes for 35 years. But she was in an attitude of prayer for 35 years, and then one day when her husband was in his seventies he received Christ and stepped into the kingdom of God. God hears our prayers!

The Right Approach

As we approach God in prayer we first need to praise Him, to adore Him, to thank Him for all the things He has given us. This is better than asking God immediately for all the things we want.

Then we need to confess our sins and shortcomings to God, opening up our heart and talking freely to God.

We should be willing to thank God for everything. Our attitude should be one of thankfulness. If we're depressed, we should thank God for even the smallest things. As we begin to make a list of the things that we're thankful for, our selfishness will begin to disappear.

Then we need to submit ourselves to God. He wants to hear our needs and our supplications. Matthew 7:7,8 says, "Ask, and it shall be given to you; seek, and you shall find; knock, and it shall be opened to you. For everyone who asks receives, and he who seeks finds, and to him who knocks it shall be opened." God *wants* to answer our prayer, to give us the desires of our heart.

Make a List

When you organize your prayer notebook you need to make a list of the things you would like to pray for. For example, you could have a section for your family. Then you could have personal prayer requests. These could include such things as financial needs or a situation between you and your husband.

You should also have a section in your notebook for your church, including your pastor and his wife and family. All of us should pray for the rulers of our country, our state, and our city. If you have children in school you should pray for the principal and all the teachers, plus the friends that your children have at school.

And then of course you should pray for yourself. Pray that you can begin to incorporate some of the organization that we've talked about. Pray for your personal needs. You may be struggling with anger over someone or selfishness or whatever it is.

And you need to pray for your husband. It is important that you uphold him in prayer. He's out there working, struggling in the world, trying to make a living. Situations and circumstances come into his life that require you to uphold him and support him in prayer.

And then of course we need to pray for our missionaries as they spread God's Word to many different people throughout the world in areas that we ourselves cannot reach.

Keeping Track

As we take this list of items that we're to pray for, we delegate them in our notebook to our little tabs. The tabs will be labeled with each day of the week. This is the easiest way I have found to set up a prayer notebook. So you have Monday, Tuesday, Wednesday, Thursday, Friday, Saturday and Sunday tabs.

Behind the Monday tab you might put your family prayer requests, listing those people in your family that you're to pray for. So when Monday morning comes and you have your little quiet time with the Lord, you pray for those needs, so that you know they're being covered at least once a week. (Of course you can pray for them at other times as well.)

Tuesday might be your prayer day for your country, your church, your pastor, and maybe your Bible study. Bob and I teach a Tuesday night couples' Bible study, so we have under my Tuesday tab the needs of the couples in our study. During the study I list the prayer requests that are given. This way I can look on the page and see that Peter doesn't have a job. So I pray for Peter. Then when Peter gets a job I say, "Thank You, Lord, for giving Peter a job." (Always date your prayer requests and answers.)

Saturday is a difficult day, so I make it miscellaneous. Sometimes on Saturday you may not even get to praying. Your children are home, your scheduling is off, and you're going on picnics and so forth. So keep Saturday open.

On Sunday, instead of having a list of people I pray for, I outline the sermons. I find that if I'm writing, I'm listening better, and I'm able to understand the sermon better and digest it better. I also find that people come to me with prayer requests at church on Sunday. So I write these in my prayer notebook on Sunday, and I pray for them on Monday, Tuesday, Wednesday, or Thursday as I'm going through my time of prayer during the week.

God Hears the Children Too

Give your children an opportunity to share in prayer with you also. Let them give you some prayer requests. Bob and I started doing this when our children were in high school. Since breakfast was the only meal of the day when we would gather together as a family, we would share with one another at that time. For example: "What kind of exam are you going to have?" After we got together again we would always have a point of reference: "How did your exam go?" They might say to me, "How did your speaking go?" Or they might ask "How was your job today? Did you get the project done that you were working on?" This way prayer requests become part of our lives.

When to Pray

When should we pray? The morning is an important time to pray. Maybe we can pray in a private place in our home. Or maybe it could be somewhere else. I spend a lot of time in my car, and I find this a valuable time to spend in prayer. People look at me on the street or the freeways and wonder why nobody else is in the car and my mouth is moving. But I'm talking to my Lord. Be sure not to close your eyes when you're driving and praying!

We also need to pray with other people. Matthew 18:20 says, "Where two or three have gathered together in My name, there I am in their midst" (NASB). As we pray together, we don't need to make our prayers long, praying for everything in the world and everything in our notebook. I have found that women who pray that way generally don't have good prayer time to themselves at home because they spend so much time when they're with someone else with these long, flowery prayers. God doesn't care about our words; he only cares about our attitude.

We can pray short prayers in our Bible study group, in our prayer group, or over the telephone. Often people call me with a problem and I say, "Let's pray." This is a wonderful way to spend some time on the phone. I don't have a lot of time for deep conversation on the phone, but I take the time to say, "Let's pray about it. I don't know all the details of your situation, and you don't have to spell them all out to me, but God knows all about them, so let's pray about it."

The Desires of Our Heart

God is interested in the desires of our heart, even the "I'd love to have it but I'm afraid to ask because it may seem selfish or even a little silly." It's the *attitude* about those things that He's really concerned about.

Check yourself by saying, "Lord, if it wouldn't be good for me to have them, then I really don't want them. But if it would be okay with You, I'd be very grateful and would use it for Your glory." Your list could include a lot of things; these are prayer wishes. Maybe it's a new sofa, or the women's overnight retreat that you can't attend because you don't have the finances.

I have a friend whose curling iron went out, but she didn't have enough money to buy a new iron. (She wanted a thin one.) So she went into a beauty supply store and told the man that she didn't have any money but needed a curling iron. He replied, "Don't worry about it—we have one that was brought back because the lady didn't want a thin one. She didn't have it in the right box, so you can have it." My friend couldn't believe that God was even interested in her curling iron!

So remember to thank God for all things, because He is interested all things. Ephesians 5:20 says, "Always give thanks for all things in the name of our Lord Jesus Christ." God is interested in the desires of our heart.

One Set of Footprints

One night a man had a dream. In his dream he was walking along the beach with the Lord, when across the sky flashed all the things of his life. However, for each scene he noticed two sets of footprints in the sand, one belonging to him and the other to the Lord. When the last scene had flashed before him, he looked back at the footprints and noticed that many times along the path there was only one set of footprints in the sand. He also noticed that this happened during the lowest and saddest times of his life.

This really bothered him, so he said to the Lord, "You promised that once I decided to follow You, You would walk with me all the way, but I noticed that during the roughest times of my life there was only one set of footprints. I don't understand why You deserted me when I needed You the most." The Lord replied, "My precious child, I love you and I would never leave you. During those times of trial and suffering when you saw only one set of footprints, it was then that I carried you."

You see, God is always with us. When the times are the lowest, that's when He picks us up and carries us. Isn't that wonderful? Some of us have experienced that. Some of us right now are in a position where we're being carried through a rough situation or problem in our life. It's wonderful to know that we have our Lord there in order to carry us when times get low and things get rough.

Prayer Organization Outline
Devote yourselves to prayer, keeping alert in it with an attitude of thanksgiving.
(Colossians 4:2 NASB)

MATERIALS NEEDED
- Small 3-ring binder with front pocket
- Paper
- 7 dividers with tabs
- Pen
- Bible

WHY PRAY?
A. Our Lord prayed. "*He walked away, perhaps a stone's throw, and knelt down and prayed this prayer: 'Father, if you are willing, please take away this cup of horror from me. But I want your will, not mine.' Then an angel from heaven appeared and strengthened him, for he was in such agony of spirit that he broke into a sweat of blood, with great drops falling to the ground as he prayed more and*

more earnestly. At last he stood up again and returned to the disciples—only to find them asleep, exhausted from grief" (Luke 22:41-45 TLB).

B. Confession.
C. Discipline.
D. Draws us closer to our Lord.
E. Praying for others keeps us from selfishness.
F. Helps us to love those we have difficulties loving.
G. Keeps us from disobedience to God and temptations.

"God will provide the way of escape"
(1 Corinthians 10:13).

"Pray God that you will not fall when you are tempted"
(Luke 22:46 TLB).

HOW TO PRAY
He knelt down and began to pray
(Luke 22:41 NASB).

A. *"Don't recite the same prayer over and over as the heathen do, who think prayers are answered only by repeating them again and again. Remember, your Father knows exactly what you need even before you ask him"* (Matthew 6:7,8 TLB).

B. A Helpful Reminder
  A - Adore God.
  C - Confess to God.
  T - Thank God for everything.
  S - Supplication and submission unto God.

C. *"Ask, and it shall be given to you; seek, and you shall find; knock, and it shall be opened to you. For everyone who asks receives, and he who seeks finds, and to him who knocks it shall be opened"* (Matthew 7:7,8 NASB).

WHAT TO PRAY FOR

A. Make a list of all needs:
   1. Family (children, in-laws, etc.)
   2. Personal (finances, problems)
   3. Friends
   4. Church (pastor and his family, church leaders)
   5. Country (city, state, president, etc.)
   6. School (teachers, principal, students)
   7. Husband (work, etc.)
   8. Self (home, anger, organizing, etc.)
   9. Missionaries

Delegate the above to a day of the week, Monday through Saturday (use tabs).

B. Sunday's tab will be used for sermon outlines and prayer requests.
   1. Prayer requests will be added to the above categories.
   2. Date prayer requests of others and date God's answers. Answers may be a wait (not now), no, or yes. Always give thanks.

C. Let the children give prayer requests. *"All things you ask in prayer, believing, you shall receive"* (Matthew 21:22 NASB).

WHEN TO PRAY

• Morning *"Seek first the kingdom of God and His righteousness, and all these things be added unto you"* (Matthew 6:33).

• Noon

• Evening

- Meals
- Bedtime

WHERE TO PRAY
*When you pray, go into your inner room,
and when you have shut your door, pray to your
Father who is in secret, and your Father who sees in
secret will repay you.* (Matthew 6:6 NASB)

A. Home—closet, dishes, vacuum, cleaning.
B. In the car, jogging, exercising, walking.
C. With others— *"Where two or three have gathered
   together in my name, there I am in their midst"*
   (Matthew 18:20 NASB).
   1. Bible study groups
   2. Women's prayer groups
   3. With a girlfriend
   4. Phone

WISH PRAYERS
A. God already knows the desires of our hearts, and He
   wants us to ask Him for them. It's the *attitude* about
   those things that He is concerned about.
B. Check yourself by saying, "Lord, if it wouldn't be
   good for me to have them, then I really don't want
   them. But if it would be okay with You, I'll be very
   grateful and use it for Your glory."
C. Be prepared. God always answers. It may be an im-
   mediate yes, a wait awhile, an absolute no, or the
   timing is not right at present. Record these answers
   in your notebook by the item, and allow God to
   work in your life with His love in giving you what's
   best for your life. Remember to thank Him in all
   things. *"Always giving thanks for all things in the
   name of our Lord Jesus Christ"* (Ephesians 5:20
   NASB).

12
HOW TO GIVE A PIGGY PARTY

A piggy party is basically a theme. You want to make it as much fun as you possibly can, not only for yourself but also for your guests. To get started you'll need the proper materials. You'll need a pink sheet or pink tablecloth. (Or you could take a white sheet and dye it pink.) You'll also want to get matching pink napkins.

Your invitations can be made up on brown construction paper. Take grocery bags and cut them open to show the inside—just plain brown paper. Don't use anything really nice and fancy, because that's not the way piggies are. Then buy some pink piggy stickers (or make them from pink construction paper), and put the piggies on your invitations. Do the same thing for your nametags. You may also want to buy an apron with pigs on it or else make your own piggy apron.

You'll want everybody to wear pink. That should be a necessity. When you send out the invitations, have them read, "Please wear pink." Have some pink shirts handy in case somebody decides to come to your party without wearing pink. You could also, make some type of pink piggy hats for your guests.

MENU

Pink Ripple Punch Cocktail

* * *

Greens and Hog Rind (Spinach Salad)

* * *

Porky Bread (Corn Bread)

* * *

Sausage Slop

* * *

Mud Pie

* * *

Leftover Coffee and Tea

(All recipes serve 8-12 guests)

Pink Ripple Punch Cocktail

Mix 1 part Fresca with 1 part cranberry juice cocktail.
Add lots of ice and a sprig of mint, if available.

Greens and Hog Rind

1 or 2 bunches spinach—clean, rinse and spin out
¼ lb. mushrooms sliced thin
bacon bits (fresh or in the jar)
1 cup bean sprouts
sliced red onion
2 hard-boiled eggs, grated or chopped
bottle of Lawry's Canadian Bacon Salad Dressing

In a large bowl place greens. Add bean sprouts, onion, mushrooms, hard-boiled eggs, and bacon bits. Toss with salad dressing.

Porky Bread

1 cup fresh cornmeal
1 cup whole wheat flour (can be white)
1 egg
4 tsp. baking powder
1 tsp. salt
¼ cup honey
¼ cup oil
1 cup milk

Mix and bake in a greased square pan at 425° for 20-30 minutes.

Sausage Slop

12 hot Italian sausages
2 or more yellow squashes
3 or more summer squashes
1 eggplant—peel and dice into medium pieces
1 lb. fresh mushrooms (quartered)
2 green peppers—cut into medium pieces
2 zucchini, sliced
2 large canned whole tomatoes

Leave sausages whole and brown very well in a skillet. In a large pot, put all other ingredients with the 2 cans of whole tomatoes. Add seasonings and sausage (garlic salt; Lawry's Seasoned Salt). Bring to a boil and simmer 2-3 hours. Serve in large bowls with 1-2 sausages per person. Oink, Oink good!

Mud Pie

½ package Nabisco chocolate wafers
½ cube butter, melted
1 quart coffee ice cream
1½ cups fudge sauce
Whipped cream
Slivered almonds

Crush wafers and add butter; mix well. Press into 9"
pie plate. Cover with soft coffee ice cream. Put into
freezer until ice cream is firm. Top with cold fudge
sauce (it helps to place in freezer for a time to make
spreading easier). Store in freezer approximately 10
hours. Slice mud pie into eight portions and serve on a
chilled dessert plate with a chilled fork. Top with
whipped cream and slivered almonds.

Compliments of "The Chart House" Restaurant

Centerpiece

leafy spinach
red leaf lettuce
cabbage
corn-on-the-cob (if available)
radishes with tops
mushrooms
carrots with tops
green onions
bamboo skewers
9" x 13" Pyrex dish or flat-type basket

Food and Fun

Your centerpiece should be made up of things that
pigs like. This is a fun opportunity to show your

creativity. Every time you make the centerpiece it could turn out a little different. You need a basket, plus a Pyrex dish or bowl to put inside the basket, plus two inches of water inside the bowl to keep the vegetables fresh. You'll also need some long bamboo skewers. (You can buy them in the market.) A head of cabbage is placed first on the bottom of the bowl. Lettuce greens go around the inside edges of the basket. (You might also use parsley, spinach, turnips, carrots with greens left on, etc.—anything leafy that pigs like.) Into your basic head of cabbage or lettuce should go skewers loaded with carrots, radishes, mushrooms, brussels sprouts, green peppers, tomatoes, etc.

If you're going to have a potluck, take the recipes provided in this book and make them available to the people who are bringing things (so that everybody has the same menus). For instance, if you're going to have the pink ripple punch, have some people bring the Fresca and some other people bring the cranberry juice. You provide the ice and the punch bowl.

The sausage slop is your main dish, and it is absolutely delicious. It's very simple to make, too. It just has the sausage and a lot of vegetables. Don't leave anything out that's shown on the recipe—it's all important.

You won't believe how cute your party looks when everyone wears pink. All your guests will think it's a great idea, and they'll probably even want to do piggy parties of their own.

But the most important thing in all this is not just to be able to put on a well-organized piggy party, but to become the organized and creative woman that God wants you to be. He wants you to be touched by the power of the Holy Spirit as you minister Christ to other people. As Jesus said in Matthew 6:33, "Seek ye first the kingdom of God and His righteousness, and all these things will be added to you as well."

How to Give a Piggy Party

MATERIALS NEEDED

Tablecloth . . . A pink sheet or a printed pink sheet or a white sheet you can dye pink.

Napkins . . . . . Matching the cloth or paper napkins with pigs on them.

Invitations . . . Dirty beige construction paper and piggy stickers.

Nametags . . . . Dirty beige construction paper and piggy stickers.

Menu . . . . Provided.

Centerpiece . . Lots of greens and vegetables.

PLEASE WEAR PINK!

YOU'RE INVITED
TO A
PINK PIGGY PARTY

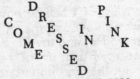

COME DRESSED IN PINK

When: February 27, 1982
Slop Time: 6:00 P.M.
Pigpen: Barnes' Place
R.S.V.P.: Regrets only!
We're going to have
an Oink of a time!

Piggy Game Instructions

EQUIPMENT NEEDED

1. Enough tables and chairs for a multiple of 4-6 players at each table.
2. Pen or pencil for each player.
3. One die for each table.
4. Each player to have one pink game sheet.

OBJECTIVE

To roll the die quick enough to draw the pig with all parts drawn. When this is done, the person with the completed pig yells out *piggy!* This constitutes the end of the game.

DIRECTIONS

1. By looking at the game sheet, you will notice that the pig has a body, a head, two ears, two eyes, a tail, and four legs.
2. Each of the parts may be drawn by the proper roll of the die. In order to draw the body for each game, the player must roll a (1) first. After the body is drawn, you may add tail and legs, but you must roll a (2) for the head before you can draw the ears (3) or eyes (4).
3. To determine who starts the roll for each game at each table, each player at each table rolls the die. The player with the highest number on the die is first to roll when the game begins.
4. When all players are ready to roll the die, the host or hostess will call out "OINK, OINK." The game begins.

5. In a clockwise direction, each player rolls the die until he or she has a (1) on the die. Then they draw the shape of the pig's body on the space given for that game.

6. You may not draw any other parts of the pig's anatomy until the body has been drawn. However, you may draw the tail and legs before you have the head drawn.

7. After the body is drawn, you must roll a (2) for the head before you can draw the ears (3) or eyes (4).

8. After the body has been drawn, the player gets a second roll if he/she rolls a (6).

9. The first player to complete all parts of the pig yells out *piggy!* This completes the game. All players total their scores for the game and write the amount on the total line for that game. (If a person yells *piggy* and doesn't have all the parts drawn, 10 points are deducted from that game's total, and you continue until someone properly yells *piggy*.)

10. The person with the highest score for each game advances to the next table, and the loser from table 1 starts back to the last table. (Number your tables 1,2,3,4, etc.)

11. The game continues in this fashion until the total games are completed. (You may shorten the number of games if you wish.)

12. Have all players total all the games to arrive at the grand total.

13. Have door prizes for the winner and loser. Select appropriate prizes that relate to pigs—e.g. sausage, bacon, corn, etc.

14. HAVE A GREAT EVENING OF FUN!

Die Roll—Points

1 - BODY = 1   5 - TAIL = 5
2 - HEAD = 2   6 - LEGS = 24
3 - EAR = 6   Total 46
4 - EYE = 8

Game 1	Game 2
Total ____	Total ____
Game 3	Game 4
Total ____	Total ____
Game 5	Game 6
Total ____	Total ____
Game 7	Game 8
Total ____	Total ____
Game 9	Game 10
Total ____	Total ____

Appendixes

Appendix 1

Sample Daily Routine

A. *Start your day the night before.*
   > *She is energetic, a hard worker, and watches for bargains. She works far into the night!*
   > (Proverbs 31: 17,18 TLB)

   - Gather wash and sort it.
   - Set breakfast table.
   - Lay out vitamins in individual cups.
   - Make orange juice.
   - Set up coffeepot for morning.
   - Make list of what must be done next day.

B. *Get up early.*
   > *She gets up before dawn to prepare breakfast for her household, and plans the day's work for her servant girls.*
   > (Proverbs 31:15 TLB)

   - Make the bed, one side at a time.
   - Put on a decent robe or attractive clothes.
   - Do at least a light makeup job and hair combing.
   - Put in first load of wash.

C. *Advance to the kitchen.*
   > *She watches carefully all that goes on throughout her household, and is never lazy.*
   > (Proverbs 31:27 TLB)

   - Rejoice that the table is set and attractive.
   - Cook breakfast and put out butter, milk, etc.
   - Call everyone to table with two-minute warning.
   - Serve all at once and sit down. (Don't be a short order cook.)

154/More Hours In My Day

- Remind everyone to take vitamins.
- Review each person's day, noting where you are needed.
- Have everyone take their dishes to the sink.
- Quickly put away all perishables.
- Put all dishes in the sink to soak in hot water.

D. *Say farewell to the family.*
   When she speaks, her words are wise, and kindness
   is the rule for everything she says.
   (Proverbs 31:26 TLB)
- See if husband has any needs.
- Check each child's room with him.
- See that bed is made and clothes hung up or in wash.
- Check bathroom for clothes and for cleanliness.
- Check to see that each one has lunch, money, books, homework, gym clothes, etc.
- Compliment them on how well they have done something.
- Send them off with a loving hug.
- Help them to remember you as a smiling mother and not a screaming shrew.

E. *Get back to work.*
   She is energetic, a hard worker.
   (Proverbs 31:17 TLB)
- Put in a second load of wash.
- Do the dishes.
- Do any advance dinner preparation—brown hamburger for casserole, cook rest of bacon for future use, make a dessert, prepare jello, etc.
- Clean up the counters.
- Water the houseplants.

- Rejoice that your basic housework is done and it's only 9 o'clock!

F. *Prepare the home for the evening.*
She watches carefully all that goes on throughout her household, and is never lazy. Her children stand and bless her; so does her husband.
He praises her with these words: There are many fine women in the world, but you are the best of them all!
(Proverbs 31:27-30 TLB)
- Light fire and candles. (Seasonal)
- Prepare munchies if dinner is a bit late: energy mix, raisins and nuts, sour cream and cottage cheese, carrot sticks, cucumber, zucchini or cauliflower.
- Set table with centerpiece.
- Prepare yourself: freshen makeup, check dress, put on perfume.
- Start thinking toward a quiet and gentle spirit.
- Organize children as best as you possibly can.
- Be ready for husband's arrival.
- Always meet him. Get yourself up and to the door with a hug, kiss, and a smile.
- Let him have ten minutes to unwind with paper or mail.
- Do not share the negative part of the day with him until after dinner.
- Enjoy your family.

Be beautiful inside, in your heart, with the lasting charm of a gentle and quiet spirit which is so precious to God.
(1 Peter 3:4 TLB)

Appendix 2

Odds and Ends

Greeting cards
- Birthday
- Baby
- Anniversary
- Sympathy
- Get well
- Thank you

Gift shelf
- Sales/toys/books

Gift wrap
- All-occasion wrap
- 3 ribbon colors
- Scotch tape
- Straw flowers
- Brown paper for mailing packages
- Mailing labels
- String
- Brown paper or strapping tape

Home office (in desk or drawer or shelf)
- Scissors
- Paper clips
- Pens/pencils
- Scotch tape
- Thank you notes
- Marking pens
- Postcards
- Roll of stamps
- Glue stick

- Rubber stamp/stamp pad
- Stationery
- Letter opener
- Memo pad
- Paperweight
- String
- Dictionary
- Paper/3x5 cards
- File box and colored folders (see 5-week program)

Items to keep near telephone
- Card file for address book
  (write information in pencil)
- Pens/pencils (in box or juice can)
- Scissors/nail file/letter opener (in box or juice can)
- Memo pad
- Calling card file/folder
- Emergency telephone numbers

Your own business cards!
- Use your talents!

Student	Handmade dolls
Jogger	Ceramics
Seamstress	Quilts/pillows
Wife/mother	Whole wheat bread
Nurse	Organizer

Auto Supplies (for glove compartment/trunk)
- Flashlight
- Maps
- Can opener
- Dimes
- Reading material
- Business cards
- Band-aids

- Matches
- Stationery/postcards
- Pen/pencil
- Blanket/towel
- Scissors/nail clippers
- Fuses
- Rope
- Jumper cables
- Flares/first aid kit
- Hide-A-Key (extra set in house)

For more information regarding speaking engagements and additional material for More Hours In My Day, please address all correspondence to:

MORE HOURS IN MY DAY
2838 Rumsey Drive
Riverside, California 92506